Praise for *Cultivating Culture*

"Wow! Brad draws you in like a bear to honey. I couldn't stop reading as I faced the mirror and answered the tough questions he poses about our core values and culture. Does our culture really help people rise above themselves and reach their full potential? Are we walking the talk or just creating confusion? Hmmmm. I knew I had better read on. Thank you Brad for the nudge to work on our core values and culture, the glue that holds us together. We can do better, and we will."

—Daphne Large, CEO, Data Facts, Inc.

"I have had the pleasure of working with Brad for many years. He has become a tremendous thought partner as well as a friend. I've watched him break down teams only to build them back up by tapping into potential they would never have realized without his artful guidance. For those who've had the pleasure of taking this journey with him, that untapped potential is sustainable. *Cultivating Culture* is a playbook to help leaders take that path themselves. Brad provides simple steps, provoked by thoughtful questions, to yield honest insights. You don't roll out a culture; it's earned through dedication and commitment. Your teams deserve this. Enjoy the adventure."

—Rick Colling, Global Head, Homewood Suites by Hilton

"Brad has been a trusted advisor for many years. *Cultivating Culture* is a road map for business leaders to use to help navigate their way through the difficult challenge of improving culture. Brad provides a tangible guide that outlines simple solutions leaders can follow to make a measurable impact on culture. This book, combined with intention and commitment, will serve as a catalyst any leader needs to foster new relationships with their employees."

—B. Scot Lenoir, Chairman Evolve Bank & Trust

"Whether you are a new manager of people or have years of experience, successful leadership involves continuous learning and improvement. It's important to refine your approaches and find new tools and methods to help your company's culture flourish. *Cultivating Culture* provides proven, practical activities to improve communication and two-way dialog. The book includes templates for conversation and exploration to help managers navigate the cultural changes occurring in today's workforce. Include it in your library for reference and refer to it often to keep your skills sharpened and teams engaged."

—Lani Glancy, Vice President, Talent Development, DEI and Communications, AutoZone, Inc.

"To be truly impactful, corporate culture must be tightly intertwined into the fabric of an organization. In *Cultivating Culture*, Brad Federman lays out practical and actionable methods for leaders to continuously instill and support company culture within their everyday meetings and workplace projects. Leaders will benefit by having this book as a trusted resource for building and maintaining stronger connections within their organizations."

—Rick Fogelman, CEO Fogelman Multifamily Investments and Management

Also by Brad Federman

Employee Engagement:
A Roadmap for Creating Profits, Optimizing Performance,
and Increasing Loyalty

101 Great Ways to Enhance Your Career

Jump Start: 50 Ways to Engage Your Team

CULTIVATING

101 Ways to
Foster Engagement
in 15 Minutes or Less

CULTURE

BRAD FEDERMAN

Matt Holt Books
An Imprint of BenBella Books, Inc.
Dallas, TX

BenBella Books, Inc.
10440 N. Central Expressway
Suite 800
Dallas, TX 75231
benbellabooks.com
Send feedback to feedback@benbellabooks.com

BenBella and *Matt Holt* are federally registered trademarks.

Printed in the United States of America
10 9 8 7 6 5 4 3 2 1

Library of Congress Control Number: 2021040494
ISBN 9781637740637 (trade cloth)
ISBN 9781637740644 (ebook)

Copyediting by Michael Fedison
Proofreading by Lisa Story and Michael Fedison
Text design and composition by PerfecType, Nashville, TN
Cover design by Brigid Pearson
Cover image © Shutterstock / hobbit
Printed by Lake Book Manufacturing

To all the leaders who understand that relationships are the foundation for creating and sustaining culture. It is a daily effort.

For my wife, Hollie, whose support has allowed me to make contributions like this to my field, and my two sons, Aris and Eli, who give me a reason to strive for more and demonstrate what is possible.

Last, thank you, Mom and Dad, for always believing in me. I miss you, Dad.

► CONTENTS

► FOREWORD

Ed McGee, EVP Operations at Fender Music Corporation
and Co-President of Fender Play Foundation

H*ad I met another people whisperer this soon?*
The transition from Harley-Davidson to ABB in early 2014 was everything I expected. A tad bit scary, a tad bit exhilarating, but most of all, the sheer joy of newness that lifelong learners experience when they jump into the deep end of a new company and new set of experiences.

I'll admit, I was a bit full of myself when it came to the topics of culture and transformation. We had just pulled off what was thought to be the impossible task of transforming a factory steeped in a culture of rugged individualism. The path to IndustryWeek Best Plants in 2014 was lined with blood, sweat, and more than a couple of tears—required ingredients of any worthwhile endeavor. But this experience was special for me because I truly cut my teeth on the hard work required to understand, evaluate, and endure the work required of leaders when they engage in cultural transformation.

Brad's smile and affable southern mannerism put me at ease. He nodded as I repeated the story of our cultural journey in York, Pennsylvania—a story that I had told thousands of times to visitors, customers, and employees alike. Culture change is hard work, I explained to him. Then he smiled and asked, "How is this story different than Harley-Davidson and why does that matter?"

I sat there stunned, thinking to myself, *Have I just met another people whisperer?* And, indeed, as I would learn from many more years of working with Brad, not only is he a practiced people whisperer, but he's also one of those unique individuals so grounded in people and culture that my learning in this space was beginning all over again.

Cultivating Culture is a book for leaders struggling with the gap between the oft-repeated values of their organizational culture and the reality of the untended cultural garden that exists in so many companies. Brad has always been an advocate of Edgar Schein's hypothesis that leaders are simply *creators of culture.** But like any great leadership outcome, culture requires exploration, reflection, and daily purpose to align what organizations want from their culture and what their organizations reflect in the daily behaviors of their employees.

Brad's gift is the ability to take what's ambiguous, uncertain, and murky and create actionable, purposeful activities that create stronger relationships between leaders and the people that they serve. Where organizations don't need help on the next set of amazing metrics that will surely drive transformative business success, those same organizations tend to be woefully inadequate in developing an equally introspective set of tasks that create and drive sustainable culture change. If you're even remotely unsure of where your organization is with respect to implementing tools of culture change, then this book is a *must read* for your leadership team.

After three wonderful years in Memphis, I packed up my bags and headed out West to Fender Musical Instruments Corporation, where their new CEO was in the process of building a leadership team to drive

---

* Edgar Schein, *Organizational Culture and Leadership* (Wiley, 2016).

culture change and organizational transformation of one of the most storied guitar companies on the planet. Andy Mooney's simple task was this: "I want our people to grow and develop at the same rate as the business." Although I had a solid set of experiences and practices now from two organizations, it was time to put those cultural life lessons to work in a new environment.

Many of the practices that Brad espouses in *Cultivating Culture* were validated over the past four years at Fender. I engaged in many of the simple, repeatable practices that leaders must embrace to signal to the organization both the significance of culture and the work required to nurture relationships that create sustainable change. Employees want to hear from their leaders the purpose of their work—they want to engage, with their hearts and minds, in work that matters. When leaders take the time to make these connections and build upon foundations of meaning and purpose, good and sustainable business outcomes happen—I have lived it and this book lays out purposeful ways to achieve those ends.

Businesses are not capable of emotion, love, connection, and purpose. Leaders take their employees on journeys that either affirm or destroy connection to mission, vision, and purpose. This takes intentional work! I hope you enjoy Brad's exploration of this intentional work as much as I did. People whisperers are indeed rare birds, but when you find one, take the time to enjoy their songs. Your employees and business will benefit greatly from both the exploration and commitment to cultivating cultures that bring meaning and purpose to work and life.

► INTRODUCTION

I have walked through the halls of countless companies seeing posters on the walls and placards on desks espousing beautifully written values. I have perused websites that elegantly express the culture within that organization only to experience and observe a completely different reality existing within the figured walls of those organizations.

Culture and values, just like the mission of a company, must live and be experienced regularly, if not every day. They must be known and part of the company DNA. Culture and values influence the way we work, the decisions we make, and the way we treat one another in good and, more importantly, in difficult times.

Culture and values are bigger than just one person. They bind groups of people together for a common goal or effort and help people rise above themselves. When done right, they create pride and engagement.

Culture and values must constantly be revisited. They need to be alive and active. Whether you hold shift meetings or monthly meetings, use performance appraisals, or hold coaching sessions, culture and values should be built into the operation and people threads of the business. We should measure how we are doing against them, train people on them, and brainstorm new ways to make our culture and values stay fresh and alive. We should find ways to help people identify with and personalize their approach to our culture and values.

Culture and values are the glue that holds us together as an organization and connects us with our customers. They are the vehicle that helps us all drive in the same direction.

Yet when we go to meetings and have internal discussions, culture and values are rarely highlighted. We discuss projects, tasks, deadlines, problems, and more. So much of our time is spent updating each other. People hate meetings and see them as a waste of time largely because they are poorly run and have little impact.

Think about it this way. We are what we talk about. We are what we meet about. What we express is what we value. Do your conversations at work reflect your culture and values?

To be an effective leader in today's world can sometimes be a complex and trying task. With different personalities, numerous generational differences, and sometimes conflicting agendas, trying to move a workgroup in the same direction for a common goal often may feel like pushing a rope uphill. What if there was a common denominator in being a more effective leader? What if there was a way to make your job as a leader easier without taking more time from your already busy day? What if I told you, by using the pages in this book, it would help you find the answer to leadership questions like these?

One of the standard practices in great companies is for every single workgroup to participate in a daily, weekly, or monthly culture/value stand-up or huddle. This is a great method for all the employees to receive a relevant message from their leader prior to beginning their various job functions each day, and to create two-way dialogue and a call to action that drives important aspects of the business such as service, safety, respect, trust, and more. These meetings last anywhere from just a couple of minutes to a maximum of 20 minutes. They and what is communicated in them make the difference in why some leaders are more successful than others, some teams are stronger than others, and why some brands stand out from others. This book can be utilized by trainers and human resources, but it is meant to be used by leaders and supervisors throughout an organization to spread a common message, sustain a desired culture, and drive business using productive values.

Many managers, even very tenured, struggle with some of the routine, everyday facets of the job. If you observe these leaders regularly when they interact with the frontline employees, you will notice a distinct difference in the content of these meetings. Many technically savvy managers only speak about what they are comfortable with—operational issues and planning—resulting in lower productivity and a greater number of human resource–related issues. More successful leaders not only cover the necessary operational plans, but they personalize their meetings to reach something deeper in their employees. These successful leaders use emotional intelligence in their message to gain the discretionary effort required when times become hard and employees have to dig deep to make the business successful.

What you have in this book are the ingredients to cultivate culture in 15 minutes or less during short meetings that will exponentially impact your ultimate success. The topics are divided into key areas that you will want to address, and you can easily place them on your daily/weekly/monthly meeting agendas. These pre-work meeting notes will allow you to connect with your team on a level that is sure to help each member reach their potential. The topics are written in a way that will challenge your team to take a fresh perspective on old problems, while helping remove barriers and silos within your workgroup. There is even a physical example of a meeting agenda provided after the conclusion in this book to demonstrate how culture is built and sustained with this type of an effort.

The messages in this book were purposely written to promote two-way conversation. You will deliver an activity your team will actually feel a part of. By implementing this collection into your meeting routine and adapting your meeting agenda, not only will you begin to see a difference in your team, you will also see a difference in yourself and your abilities as a leader to achieve more with less effort. Most importantly, you will see a difference in your business because of resilient relationships, which stem from employees who care about something bigger than themselves.

CHAPTER 1

LEADING INTENTIONALLY

CATEGORY ► LEADERSHIP

Purpose: To define *Lead by Example*

Time Requirement: 10 minutes

Materials Needed: Flipchart or whiteboard; markers

It is important to conduct dialogues about personal leadership, specifically leading by example. Oftentimes, the values we talk about do not align with our actions. Company values inform and fuel company culture. If we are not "walking the talk," we run the risk of creating confusion at best and hypocrisy at worst. This activity creates a space where teams can not only discuss their values but identify how they can better live them. Bringing the conceptual into a literal space first requires a dialogue. There is no better way to strengthen a culture than to proactively role-model the behaviors you want to see. Explore how your team can better be the role models they desire to be by leading by example.

Directions

1. What do you think the term *Lead by Example* means?
2. Why are the examples we set through our behavior sometimes stronger than what we say?

3. A popular phrase these days is "walk the talk." What does that mean?
4. Do we "walk the talk" here?
5. What can we do to "walk the talk"?
6. Facilitate and debrief the discussion by using the **Key Questions** and **Key Points** that follow.

Key Questions

- Why do we want to lead by example?
- Who is observing us and what kind of impression is it leaving?
- What happens if we don't lead by example?

Key Points

Ways to lead by example include:

- Create a second home and a second family culture.
- Actively listen and effectively communicate both verbally and nonverbally.
- Remember that you are being observed.
- What you do can be more important than what you say.

Tips/Examples/Variations

- A variation is to have them think about someone they know who leads by example. Have them use that example to think about the questions in the next activity.

CATEGORY ► **LEADERSHIP**

Purpose: To identify effective leadership behaviors

Time Requirement: 15 minutes

Materials Needed: Flipchart or whiteboard; markers

Say you want to hit a target with an arrow. To hit that bull's-eye, you must first see the target. It seems like common sense, but oftentimes people find themselves jumping toward a goal without specifying their target or how to get there. To be better leaders, we must identify leaders we would like to emulate. Moreover, we must identify what qualities make those role models such strong leaders. Who is an effective leader? What makes them so effective and inspiring? How can we conduct ourselves similarly? This is our target and, once identified, we can draw the bow.

Directions

1. Ask the participants to think of one person they believe is an effective leader. It can be someone famous or someone they know at work or in their personal life.
2. Ask the group to share three examples of effective leadership behaviors on the job.
3. Debrief the discussion by using the **Key Questions** and **Key Points** that follow.

Key Questions

- What behaviors are important for leaders to exhibit?
- Why do you think these are leadership behaviors or characteristics?

Key Points

- Looking at people we admire as leaders helps us think about how we want to behave.
- To become great leaders, we must identify the behaviors that make them great.
- Good leaders are memorable and can make a lasting impression and example in our lives and in the lives of others.
- When we exhibit good leadership behaviors, we are setting an example for others.

Tips/Examples/Variations

Examples of behaviors of effective leaders:

- Follows through on commitments.
- Displays honest and authentic behavior.
- Communicates a vision and strategy that all understand.

CATEGORY ▶ LEADERSHIP

Purpose: To discuss the phrase *Actions Speak Louder Than Words*

Time Requirement: 15 minutes

Materials Needed: Flipchart or whiteboard; markers

Trust is the cornerstone of a healthy company culture. Without it, communication breaks down, projects do not get completed, and divisions form. Strong leaders establish trust with the rest of the team. What is the best way to foster trust? Making sure that your actions align with your words. It might seem self-explanatory, but the frequency with which actions and sentiments do not align within companies can be startling. Actions speak louder than words. This activity shines a light on areas in which actions and sentiments may not be in agreement. More importantly, it allows the group to see the importance of actions. Leading by example—it is the path to establish credibility and productive communication.

Directions

1. Ask the group to describe a situation when their actions spoke louder than their words.
2. Choose one or two examples and ask the team member who gave the example to describe how their actions led to a more positive outcome.
3. Ask the team for any examples where their words were not followed by actions. Discuss.

Key Questions

- Why is what we do more powerful than what we say?
- What happens if we don't follow through on what we say?

Key Points

- People judge us based on our actions.
- Don't just say it, show it.
- Good leaders follow through on what they say. They take action.
- Sometimes taking action is the only way to get things done.

Tips/Examples/Variations

Examples of "Actions speak louder than words":

- Behaving in a customer-oriented way such as opening the door or offering to help carry luggage, rather than just using words.
- Taking initiative to help other team members rather than just telling others to do it.

CATEGORY ▶ LEADERSHIP

Purpose: To practice taking initiative

Time Requirement: 10 minutes

Materials Needed: None

What does it mean to take initiative? Why is it a strong leadership behavior? When there is no initiative present in a team, goals are never reached. A leader needs to be willing to take that first, fateful step toward a goal to get the ball rolling. Initiative is not only being willing to act but being willing to bring the rest of the team with you. Acts of initiative can be big or small, but practicing initiative is an integral part of creating an action-oriented culture. When everyone—not just leaders—is willing to take initiative, organizations can soar!

Directions

1. Ask the group what it means to "take initiative."
2. Ask why that is a leadership behavior.
3. Discuss how we can take initiative in our jobs.
4. Ask the group to find an opportunity today to take initiative.

Key Questions

- What does "take initiative" mean?
- Why is that a strong leadership behavior?
- What would happen if we worked in an environment where no one took initiative?

Key Points

- Taking initiative means being proactive, addressing problems first, doing things without being asked.
- Good leaders don't sit back and wait for things to happen; they MAKE things happen.

Tips/Examples/Variations

Examples of taking initiative:

- Picking up a piece of garbage on the floor or outside the building.
- Offering to work on a project that no one else wants to do.

CATEGORY ► **LEADERSHIP**

Purpose: To practice ethical behavior

Time Requirement: 15 minutes

Materials Needed: Flipchart or whiteboard; markers

Ethics are the foundational pillar on which a healthy company culture stands. When we hold ourselves (and subsequently our company) to a quality ethical standard, we set the foundations of trust and high expectations. It distinguishes that there is a right way and a wrong way to conduct business. Honesty promotes hard work, clear communication, and pride in the business. As a result, it is best to establish firm ethical standards for the entire team and then analyze them as a group. The following activity uses a scenario to foster an open-ended discussion about ethics.

Directions

1. Tell the group that recently a cab driver found $100,000 worth of diamonds left in a bag in his cab.
2. Ask the group what they would do if they were the cab driver. Why?
3. Ask the group what they would do if they observed something unethical or dishonest on the job.
4. Debrief by using the **Key Questions** and **Key Points** that follow.

Key Questions

- What would you do if you were the cab driver?
- Why do you think the cab driver returned the diamonds?
- What do you think the owner expected would happen?
- What would you do if you noticed unethical behavior on the job?

Key Points

- The cab driver said he couldn't live with himself if he didn't find the owner.
- The owner appreciated the return but was not expecting it.
- Addressing dishonesty or unethical behavior on the job is good corporate behavior and fosters high expectations.

Tips/Examples/Variations

- A variation is to use a local story that has been in the papers illustrating a choice that a person had to make around an ethical issue, or an ethical issue that was raised in the workplace recently. Use a company-related story if possible.

CATEGORY ► LEADERSHIP

Purpose: To practice dealing with difficult people

Time Requirement: 10 minutes

Materials Needed: Flipchart or whiteboard; markers

People disagree. Sometimes they are customers; sometimes they are members of our own team. These disagreements and issues are not always justified either. Difficult people are a reality of customer service and team-oriented projects. As such, conflict resolution is a staple of leadership and professionalism. How can a situation be resolved? What is the best way to address issues with difficult people? Composure and understanding are essential in de-escalating these situations. This exercise aids in analyzing conflict de-escalation through the lens of previous experiences with difficult people. How can we learn from the past to better equip ourselves for the future?

Directions

1. Ask the group to share some of the difficult customers or team members they have dealt with.
2. Ask participants how they handled those situations.
3. Ask: "What were the results?"
4. Ask: "Could you have done something differently for better results?"
5. Debrief using **Key Questions** and **Key Points** that follow.

Key Questions

- What is a difficult customer or team member behavior you've experienced?
- What's challenging about dealing with strong emotions?
- What do you do if a customer or team member continues with difficult behavior?

Key Points

- It is important to remain calm and patient when dealing with strong emotions.
- If you face a customer or team member who is not responding, bring in your supervisor or another team member to help.
- Make sure to ask the customer or team member if they are completely satisfied with the resolution.

Tips/Examples/Variations

Examples of difficult behavior:

- Unhappy with service.
- Angry that they can't get the results that they wanted.
- Annoyed with phone/internet service.

CATEGORY ▶ LEADERSHIP

Purpose: To define what "Recognize Contributions to Our Success" means

Time Requirement: 15 minutes

Materials Needed: Flipchart or whiteboard; markers

Good leaders are nothing without an even better team. Treating your coworkers well is a surefire way to establish a healthy company culture. Part of that is giving credit where credit is due. Recognition for hard work goes a long way in helping people feel heard and appreciated. How can we make sure employees feel recognized? Do different types of recognition resonate more with specific coworkers? These are all questions to consider. Recognition cannot be properly given without knowing the people you work with. To recognize your team is to know your team.

Directions

1. Ask the group what they think "Recognize Contributions to Our Success" means.
2. Ask why recognition is so important in the workplace.
3. Ask what the workplace would be like if we didn't get acknowledged for the good work we do.
4. Ask for ideas on how we could better recognize contributions.

Key Questions

- Why do we want to recognize success?
- How can we give recognition effectively?
- How does recognition motivate us?

Key Points

- People are most engaged when they feel good about their contributions to the team's success.
- Everyone likes to be recognized in some way for their contribution.
- It's best to give the recognition immediately.
- Recognize the contribution of team members to managers.

Tips/Examples/Variations

Examples of ways to recognize others:

- Have a group pizza party.
- Write a complimentary letter or email to that team member's manager.
- Stop a team member in the hallway and thank them for something positive they did.

CATEGORY ▶ LEADERSHIP

Purpose: To define the term *engagement*

Time Requirement: 10 minutes

Materials Needed: Flipchart or whiteboard; markers

Teams need to be passionate about their work. Individuals must understand their role in the bigger picture and subsequently find meaning in it. They have to feel energized. This is the crux of engagement. It is important to open a discussion about engagement. It will help you better assess the levels of engagement present in your team. Moreover, it is an avenue to discuss what engagement means to individuals and how it can be boosted. Engaged employees are more productive, stick around longer, and are more fun to work with. As a result, engaged employees make for a healthy company culture.

Directions

1. Say that one goal we have is for us to feel "engaged" at work.
2. Ask for ideas as to what the term *engagement* means.
3. Ask for volunteers to share what keeps them engaged in their work.
4. Ask for ideas on how to build engagement if it is not strong.
5. Debrief using the **Key Questions** and **Key Points** that follow.

Key Questions

- What is engagement?
- What are the benefits if we are engaged in our work?
- What does it look or feel like, from the *customer's* point of view, if a staff member is/is not engaged?

Key Points

- Engagement is being energized, focused, and passionate about our work.
- Engaged employees are more productive, stay longer in their jobs, and are fun to work with.
- If we lose interest in our work over time, we can start to lose our skills and contribution to the organization.

Tips/Examples/Variations

Examples of how to build engagement if it is not strong:

- Give team members job tasks that excite them.
- Give team members projects that use their unique skills and talents.
- Allow team members to work on tasks that have importance to the organization.

CATEGORY ► **LEADERSHIP**

Purpose: To examine how familiarity doesn't always mean competency

Time Requirement: 10 minutes

Materials Needed: Paper and pens

Familiarity does not always mean competency. Just because we see something every day, or are familiar with it, does not mean that we truly understand what makes it tick or recall all the details. It can be easy to assume that we have an active handle on the world around us and our responsibilities, but there may be gaps in our knowledge and skills that we are not aware of. Therefore, it is important to practice active observation. Do not get comfortable, and always seek to improve. Try stepping back and looking at your job like it is the first time you have done it.

Directions

1. Ask: "How many pennies do you think you've had in your pockets or purse during your lifetime?" Gather responses.
2. Tell the group that the average 30-year-old has had 30,000 pennies over their lifetime.
3. Ask them, having seen so many pennies, to draw what a penny looks like—both sides.
4. After a few minutes, let them pull out their pennies and compare them with their drawings.
5. Use the **Key Questions** and **Key Points** that follow to debrief.

Key Questions

- What did you learn from this activity?
- How can we be so familiar with something but not know the details?
- How can we become more observant?

Key Points

- Just because we do or see something every day doesn't mean we know everything about it.
- Practice being observant. Step back and think about the things we do every day. We may be able to improve or learn something new.

Tips/Examples/Variations

Ways to become more observant:

- Step back and approach your job as if you were doing it for the first time.
- Offer to work with a new employee to help them and to see the job from a new perspective.
- Pretend you are a new customer doing business with us or partnering with us. What would be your impression?

CATEGORY ▶ LEADERSHIP

Purpose: To identify how our contributions connect with the success of the company

Time Requirement: 15 minutes

Materials Needed: Two large pieces of paper and a variety of colorful markers

I n order to stimulate engagement and excitement about the work people are doing, it is important that they understand how integral their role is to the success of the company. If employees do not see the bigger picture, they run the risk of feeling unimportant or as though their work is nothing more than an assignment. This has drastic impacts on motivation, happiness, and productivity. Everybody's job is important to the company's bottom line. It is important for the entire team to understand this. More importantly, it is important for the team to understand why their role is so integral.

Directions

1. Introduce the topic by saying that the things we do every day on the job have a close connection with the bottom line of the company.
2. Break the group into smaller teams. Give each team a piece of flipchart paper and assorted markers.
3. Tell the teams to draw a picture of the connection between their work and the company's financial success. Tell them to be creative! They can make pictures, use words, and/or use symbols. Give them 10 minutes.
4. Ask each team to explain their picture.

Key Questions

- What do we do in our daily work that has a direct impact on our company?
- Why is it important to remind ourselves and each other of the contributions we make?

Key Points

- Everybody's job is important to the company's bottom line.
- If we forget how our work impacts the company, it is harder to see the benefits of what we do.

Tips/Examples/Variations

- A tip is to discuss some bottom-line issues of the company before having them draw their pictures. Bottom-line issues could include: financial state of the company or statistics or information on company goals.

CATEGORY ► LEADERSHIP

Purpose: To identify our leadership behaviors

Time Requirement: 10 minutes

Materials Needed: Flipchart or whiteboard; markers

It is important to identify leadership behaviors within the context of the company. Leadership takes many forms and can look different depending on the office/organization. Who in your workplace displays strong leadership? Recognizing strong leadership in members of your team not only sets an example but encourages those behaviors in the future. Essentially, give credit where credit is due. The following activity creates a space where a conversation about leadership can be had in the context of your specific workplace and encourage even more leadership moving forward.

Directions

1. Start by choosing a team member who has recently demonstrated a leadership behavior.
2. Tell the group the specific behavior and explain how it demonstrates leadership.
3. Ask team members for examples of ways they have exhibited leadership behaviors.
4. Debrief the exercise by using the **Key Questions** and **Key Points** that follow.

Key Questions

- What is a leadership behavior you have seen in a team member recently?
- Why is it important to demonstrate leadership behaviors for our customers?

Key Points

- Leadership can help us turn dissatisfaction into exceeded expectations.
- Leadership means doing more than the minimum or just getting by.
- Leadership behaviors help us stand out from our competition.
- Leadership behaviors show our customers how much we care.

Tips/Examples/Variations

- Take a moment to praise the team member you choose as your leadership behavior example to show other team members that you notice and recognize a job well done.

CATEGORY ▶ **LEADERSHIP**

Purpose: To brainstorm ways to create a second home for us and our customers

Time Requirement: 10 minutes

Materials Needed: Flipchart or whiteboard; markers

A good home is filled with trust, communication, and collaboration. In a good home, people are comfortable. In these ways, company culture should resemble a home. Just as every home is different based on the family, companies will also have their own, individual definitions of what home means. This activity opens the gate for that conversation. Create a familial culture surrounding respect. This extends beyond employees to customers as well. It is all about building relationships. When the workplace resembles a second home, customers return or recommend your company to others and employees feel valued. Everyone needs a place where they feel safe, comfortable, and valued.

Directions

1. Say that one component of leading by example is creating a home-like environment for us and for our customers.
2. Ask: "How can we create a second home here?" Record their responses.
3. Ask: "Why do we want to create a second home here? How does it benefit us and our customers?"
4. Debrief by using the **Key Questions** and **Key Points** that follow.

Key Questions

- Why do we want to create a second home?
- How can we create a second home?

Key Points

- Leading by example includes creating a home-like and family-like environment.
- We can create a family culture by respecting each other and our customers and treating each other as we would family members.

Tips/Examples/Variations

Examples of benefits of creating a second home environment:

- Customers come back.
- Customers recommend the company to others.
- Customers have a comfortable and satisfying experience.

CATEGORY ► LEADERSHIP

Purpose: To recognize how each of us leads by example

Time Requirement: 10 minutes

Materials Needed: Flipchart or whiteboard; markers

How can each individual lead by example? Qualities such as: initiative, looking for the positives, and doing what is right over what is easy are a few ways. Leadership qualities do not apply to a single person in a team, but to all. The more each member of the team works to adopt leadership habits, the stronger the team will be as a whole. Leading by example prompts others to do the same, strengthening the group. How can we optimize our behaviors and actions to be more leadership oriented on a daily basis? This activity allows employees to review leadership skills and how we can lead by example to the benefit of the entire group and promote strong personal leadership skills.

Directions
1. Review the ways we can lead by example.
2. Ask the group to find one team member today who is "leading by example." The employee could be using positive nonverbal behavior or speaking in a tone of voice that is welcoming.
3. Tell the group to give positive feedback to that employee for leading by example.

Key Questions
- How can we lead by example?
- Why is it important to do?

Key Points

- Leading by example is doing what we say we will do.
- Leading by example is using positive body language such as smiling and using a friendly tone of voice.

Tips/Examples/Variations

Examples of leading by example:

- Taking initiative to help out when busy.
- Not complaining about a new policy or procedure.
- Looking for the positive during challenging times and what can be learned from it.
- Doing what is right, not just what is easy.

CATEGORY ▶ **LEADERSHIP**

Purpose: To practice being a hero for our customers

Time Requirement: 10 minutes

Materials Needed: Flipchart; markers

Companies revolve around service—specifically to customers. Some of the best examples of service-oriented people are our heroes. They can be real or fictional; both Superman and the local firefighter are rooted in the common quest to serve others. The company should be to the customer what our heroes are to their communities. There is great utility in analyzing what we admire about our heroes and how we can emulate their positive values. Keeping the idea of serving others at the forefront helps us stay focused on why we are here.

Directions

1. Explain to the group that we all have heroes. Our heroes may be real or imaginary.
2. Have each team member share who their hero is and why they chose them.
3. Record answers on the flipchart and note any recurring themes among the heroes chosen.
4. Ask participants how we can mirror these heroes' power to deliver excellent service and be a hero for our customers.

Key Questions

- What defines a hero?
- Who is your hero? Why are they your hero?
- What characteristics does our hero have that we can emulate or develop?

- How can we be a hero to our customers?
- What's stopping you from being a hero?

Key Points

- Heroes are people we admire because we want to be more like them in some way.
- Not all heroes have superpowers—it's what they do with the power they have that makes them special.
- We can use our heroes as role models who inspire us to greatness.

CATEGORY ► LEADERSHIP

Purpose: To discuss the difference between accountability and ownership

Time Requirement: 10 minutes

Materials Needed: Flipchart or whiteboard; markers

Accountability versus ownership. What is the difference? Accountability applies to things we are expected to do. It is repercussion oriented. Ownership, however, applies to responsibilities we assume on our own. Ownership is pride and excitement oriented. We want to take ownership of our jobs, not just accountability. When we live in an ownership mindset, we are more apt to go the extra mile and invest in our responsibilities. It is *our* project. A project to be proud of, not just an expectation thrust onto us. The following exercise is designed to discuss the difference between accountability and ownership. Through it, employees may find ways that they can take ownership in their own work on a daily basis.

Directions

1. Draw a line down the middle of the flipchart, and on one side write the word "accountability"; on the other side, write "ownership."
2. Explain to the team that accountability applies to those things we are expected to do, but ownership applies to those things we assume responsibility for on our own.
3. Have each team member share something they are accountable for and something they have taken ownership of.
4. Debrief using **Key Questions** and **Key Points** that follow.

Key Questions

- How is ownership different from accountability?
- Why should we strive to take ownership at our job rather than just being accountable?
- How can we create more ownership on this team?
- How can taking ownership of a situation or task at work improve our lives outside of work?

Key Points

- Accountability relates to those things that others expect from us. We can improve customer service when we assume responsibility for solving the problems we see regardless of who is at fault. Customer service must come first.
- When we see problems, we create solutions.
- Ownership is all about attitude. We embrace opportunities and assume responsibility on our own.

Tips/Examples/Variations

- For a variation, ask for volunteers to share a time when they noticed a team member taking ownership.

CHAPTER 2

COMMUNICATING WITH PURPOSE

CATEGORY ► **COMMUNICATION**

Purpose: To brainstorm changes we can make in our processes or environment to "communicate first"

Time Requirement: 10 minutes

Materials Needed: Flipchart or whiteboard; markers

A productive relationship relies on communication. People must be comfortable asking questions and being open, both in the office and between client and company. However, communication relies on trust. One of the best ways to open the door to communication is with a strong welcome. Subsequently, there is great value in discussing welcomes. Creating a welcoming environment goes beyond simple pleasantries. It requires accessibility, transparency, and additional effort. The following exercise generates ways for employees to "communicate first" while stressing the importance of building proactive, trust-oriented relationships.

Directions

1. Introduce the topic by saying that there are things we can offer our customers, change in our processes, or change in our environment to say "welcome" and to "communicate first."
2. Share some of the examples below to get the group thinking. Encourage them to think about ways to say "welcome" beyond just saying "hello."
3. Tell the group that we're going to brainstorm to see how many ideas we can come up with.
4. Summarize the activity by discussing how these ideas can be implemented by actions you will take to help them be successful.

Key Questions

- How can we "communicate first" and show we care in our processes and procedures?
- Are there things in our environment now that are not welcoming?

Key Points

- Our environment and our processes and procedures can send a welcoming (or non-welcoming) message.
- You only get one chance to make a first impression. Make sure to connect with customers personally.

Tips/Examples/Variations

- Offer printed directions to local sites.
- Put a "welcome" sign by the entrance.
- Have extra team members available for busier hours.

CATEGORY ► COMMUNICATION

Purpose: To examine how it makes us feel when others don't "communicate first"

Time Requirement: 10 minutes

Materials Needed: Flipchart or whiteboard; markers

B e quick to the draw. Attentiveness is paramount in building relationships. By communicating first, we help the customer (internal or external) feel seen. Great service starts with acknowledgment. How can we work to ensure that customers know they have our attention and subsequently our effort? Our body language goes a long way in communicating. Little things like promptness, eye contact, and enthusiasm can make all the difference when defining a customer's perception of your business. When we do not communicate first, we show a lack of care. What keeps us from "communicating first"? This question is addressed and troubleshot in this activity, aiding employees in finding ways that they can communicate promptly and proactively.

Directions

1. Ask the group to think about a time when they were a customer and the service provider did not address them first or take initiative.
2. Ask them how they felt when this happened.
3. Ask them how that affected their relationship with that business.
4. Encourage the group to try one thing to "communicate first" today.

Key Questions

- How do we feel when people don't greet us?
- What impression do we get when the customer service providers don't "communicate first"?
- What keeps us from communicating first?

Key Points

- When others don't "communicate first," we feel ignored, unimportant, disregarded, or angry.
- By communicating first, you separate yourself from all the mediocre service providers out there.
- Ignoring customers causes businesses to create poor impressions and lose customers.
- Communicate with enthusiasm.

Tips/Examples/Variations

Examples of when customer service providers don't "communicate first":

- Bank tellers not looking at us.
- Waiters in restaurants who take too long to come to our table.
- Salespeople in stores who are doing something behind the desk rather than helping us.
- Airline staff that look the other way when they see long lines.

Purpose: To practice being approachable to our team members

Time Requirement: 10 minutes

Materials Needed: None

Have you ever needed to ask a question for clarification but felt that it would be unwelcome? Did your work suffer for it? To succeed, it is important to ask questions. This way, we can grow and develop in our positions. Nobody knows everything from the start. Therefore, it is important to create an approachable environment where collaboration and questions are encouraged. Openness is the name of the game. When people feel comfortable inquiring about their responsibilities or asking for clarification, the company succeeds. If this is suppressed, communication breaks down. People hide mistakes instead of seeking solutions. How can we be more approachable to our teammates? This activity centers around creating an environment where questions are welcome and communication can flow.

Directions

1. Say that an important component of "communicating first" is not only to start conversation but to be approachable for others to start conversation with us.
2. Ask the group why it is especially important to be approachable with our team members.
3. Ask the group for ideas on how to become more approachable (use the **Key Questions** and **Key Points** that follow to facilitate the discussion).
4. Ask the group to try one new behavior today—verbal or nonverbal—to express openness.

Key Questions

- What does being approachable mean?
- How can we show openness?
- Is being approachable important to "can do"?
- How can we improve customer service by being approachable? After all, we are in the hospitality business.
- What nonverbal behavior demonstrates openness? What verbal behavior?

Key Points

- Being approachable helps the team keep lines of communication open and helps the team function more effectively.
- Open body language—such as eye contact and smiling—can help you become more approachable.
- Closed body language—crossed arms, looking down—makes it difficult for others to approach you.
- Welcoming verbal behavior—such as "how are you" or "what's happening today"—can open the door for more conversation.

Tips/Examples/Variations

- An option is to record the ideas on the flipchart and have each team member pick one of the behaviors listed.

Purpose: To practice paraphrasing to make sure we understand the customers and each other

Time Requirement: 10 minutes

Materials Needed: Flipchart or whiteboard; markers

The purpose of communication is to understand and to be understood. One of the best feelings out there is to know that what you are attempting to communicate—be it a question, a concern, or what have you—has been heard and internalized. Paraphrasing is a highly productive way of communicating that you have internalized what has been said to you. It shows that you are listening. Being able to restate an idea in your own words shows a profound and personalized understanding of what has been said. This accomplishes what parroting cannot. You do not need to understand something to repeat it word for word. You do need to understand something to rephrase it in your own words. The following activity explains the importance of paraphrasing as well as the impact that genuinely listening can have on a workplace culture.

Directions

1. Ask the group to define what paraphrasing means.
2. Say that paraphrasing is a helpful way to make sure we understand the customer and to show that we are listening.
3. Break the group into pairs with one person acting as listener and the other as speaker.
4. Tell the speaker to share with the listener how his or her day is going today.
5. Tell the listener to find opportunities to paraphrase what the speaker said.

Key Questions
- What is paraphrasing?
- Why is it helpful to do?
- What if we paraphrase inaccurately?
- What are ways we can paraphrase effectively?

Key Points
- Paraphrasing is restating some of the key words and ideas of a speaker's message.
- Paraphrasing is NOT "parroting" a speaker word for word.
- Paraphrasing helps the speaker feel heard and helps the listener understand better.
- Paraphrasing is especially helpful in problem-solving situations.

Tips/Examples/Variations
- If time permits, have each pair switch roles so everyone has a chance to practice paraphrasing.

CATEGORY ► **COMMUNICATION**

Purpose: To practice using a positive tone of voice to "Talk It Out"

Time Requirement: 10 minutes

Materials Needed: Two index cards—one with the word *disinterested* written on it and the other with the word *friendly*

Language is complex and, oftentimes, people use more than just our words to interpret our meaning. Tone of voice plays an integral role in communicating our message. The wrong tone of voice could accidentally indicate sarcasm or disinterest, effectively killing the original intention behind your words. Believe it or not, our tone does not always sound how we think it does. Therefore, it is important to be intentional and mindful, not just about the words we say, but how we say them. This is especially important over the phone, as tone of voice is the only indicator of meaning other than the actual words we use. Phone calls lack the physical cues that people rely on to interpret meaning. Since a lot of communication occurs over the phone, tone must be paid attention to.

Directions

1. Introduce the topic by asking the group: "How important is tone of voice in a message?"
2. Say that tone of voice is an important component of a message, especially over the telephone. Say that different tones of voice can change the content of the message. For example: "You're doing a great job," said in a monotone or unenthusiastic tone of voice, might cause the listener to disbelieve what you are saying.

3. Ask for two volunteers. Give each volunteer one of the index cards and tell them not to show anyone their card.

4. Tell the volunteers you want them to demonstrate the tone of voice on their card by saying the phrase "Welcome to our company."

5. Each volunteer goes one at a time and the rest of the participants have to guess what they are feeling.

6. Debrief the exercise by using the **Key Questions** and **Key Points** that follow.

Key Questions

- Why is tone of voice so important, especially over the telephone?
- What can happen if our tone of voice is sending a different message than our words?
- How can we make sure our tone of voice is friendly and welcoming?
- Can you name a time when tone of voice swayed your opinion?

Key Points

- Tone of voice can be more important than the words we say.
- Tone of voice over the phone is 80 percent of the message.
- If our tone of voice says something different than our words, it will cause the message to be confusing, such as "Welcome" said in a low, unenthusiastic tone of voice.
- Practice improving your voice tone—smile when you speak, listen to your voicemail messages before you send them, and ask for feedback from your team members.

Tips/Examples/Variations

- Model several different tones of voice if you find the group needs help in understanding the differences.
- Have fun with this exercise! You can bring in a child's toy phone and do more than the two index cards listed. Some other tones of voice you can use are: annoyed, bored, angry, sad, indifferent, preoccupied.

CATEGORY ► COMMUNICATION

Purpose: To practice using body language to communicate first

Time Requirement: 10 minutes

Materials Needed: Six index cards, each labeled with one of the following behaviors:

Happy: You love your job

Angry: One of your team members didn't show up

Sad: You lost a big proposal

Surprised: Your colleagues recognized you at the company meeting

Tired: You pulled an all-nighter to meet a deadline

Afraid: You are scared to speak in front of the entire company

In a similar vein to tone of voice, body language also communicates a great deal to the people around us. Are we approachable? Do we look committed or like we would rather not be there? People take cues and make judgments based on our physicality. Have you ever worked with someone who looks as though they do not want to be there? Was their posture stooped? Did they avoid eye contact? How did it make you feel? People are far more likely to trust, work with, and communicate with people who carry themselves with positive and confident body language.

Directions

1. Review the concept of "communicating first" by asking the group what that means.
2. Remind the group that communicating first can be starting a conversation or it can be making it easy for a team member or customer to approach you.
3. Ask for two volunteers. Give each volunteer one index card. Tell them not to show it to anyone.
4. Tell the volunteers that they have to demonstrate the feeling/behavior written on their card only through using their bodies—no talking!
5. Tell the rest of the group to guess what they are expressing.
6. Encourage the group to use positive body language on the job.

Key Questions

- Why is it important to "communicate first"?
- What type of body language makes us more approachable?
- What negative body language do we want to avoid?
- Do you consider your body language when communicating?

Key Points

- Positive body language includes smiling or nodding, using eye contact, and keeping arms and hands open.
- Negative body language includes pointing, crossing arms, looking away, or hands on hips.
- Use positive body language to show you are ready to help and engage in conversation.

Tips/Examples/Variations

- If you have volunteers who seem lost as to how to demonstrate the behavior, you can pull them aside and coach them on what they could do to demonstrate the behavior.

CATEGORY ► COMMUNICATION

Purpose: To practice active listening

Time Requirement: 15 minutes

Materials Needed: Flipchart or whiteboard; markers

Listening and hearing are not synonyms. Hearing is passive; listening is active. To listen requires concentration and attentiveness. To listen is to internalize. When we show customers and coworkers that we are listening, we let them know that their words are important to us. This builds trust and relationships. We can show that we are actively listening through tone, body language, and rephrasing. Simple things like authentic nodding can help communicate that you are actively listening. Nobody likes being blown off. As such, we should do everything in our power to ensure that people understand that we are taking their words to heart.

Directions

1. Introduce the topic by asking the group why we don't listen at times.
2. Say that active listening requires energy and concentration.
3. Ask the group to share ways we can practice active listening such as nodding our head, paraphrasing, and eye contact.
4. Now break the group into pairs.
5. Instruct each of them to take turns sharing what they did last night. The listener should practice active listening skills.
6. Debrief the exercise by using the **Key Questions** and **Key Points** that follow.

Key Questions

- Why don't we listen?
- How does it make the speaker feel when we don't listen well?
- What are some active listening skills?
- How does it feel to be truly listened to?
- How do you think our customers feel when we don't appear to be listening?

Key Points

- Active listening is critical to building trust and authenticity.
- Active listening requires energy and specific behaviors.
- Active listening helps the customer feel cared for and heard.
- Active listening is an activity—it isn't passive.

Tips/Examples/Variations

Ways to practice active listening:

- Look the speaker in the eye.
- Say "uh-huh" to show we are listening.
- Ask questions to show we are listening and want more.

CATEGORY ► COMMUNICATION

Purpose: To practice asking for the help we need

Time Requirement: 10 minutes

Materials Needed: Flipchart or whiteboard; markers

No person is an island. At some point, even the most independent and self-sufficient people need a helping hand. This is the basis of the office. An office is a team, providing mutual aid and benefiting the growth of individuals for the betterment of the whole. However, requesting help can be a complicated, daunting, and even difficult process. Do we ask for help or are we demanding it? Are we comfortable asking for help when we need it? Creating an environment of mutual respect and clear communication goes a long way in improving workplace culture. This activity helps establish the space to ask questions while opening up a conversation about how they should be asked.

Directions

1. Ask participants to think of times during their job where they have to ask for help to accomplish a task. Record their answers on the flipchart.
2. Choose one of the scenarios given and ask the participant who offered it to explain the circumstances of the situation and role-play with another team member how they ask for help.
3. Ask the group to rate the demonstration by how the participant asked for help and to offer some suggestions to make their request more effective.
4. Debrief using **Key Questions** and **Key Points** that follow.

Key Questions

- How do we ask for help?
- When we need help, do we ask for it or do we demand it from others?
- Do we feel like we can ask for help when we need it?
- What are some of the barriers that keep us from reaching out when we need to?

Key Points

- We should expect that we can find the help we need from our team members but remember to ask for help rather than demand it.
- Strong teams offer help proactively rather than waiting to be asked.
- The best way to ensure that we get the help we need is by asking for it.

Tips/Examples/Variations

- For a variation, have team members identify examples of nonproductive ways to ask for help and ask how they felt when others addressed them in such a manner.

CATEGORY ► COMMUNICATION

Purpose: To investigate where communication breaks down

Time Requirement: 15 minutes

Materials Needed: Random objects in an open area; a blindfold

Communication is essential. However, when things get difficult, communication can break down. It is important to learn how to navigate stressful situations and regain communication during turbulent periods. Ironically, communication can be one of the first things to go when stress is on the rise. However, it is the most essential element in reducing that stress. This activity helps team members realize how complicated communication is and what they can do to improve their communication efforts.

Directions

1. Break the group into teams.
2. Have each team pick someone to navigate through the "minefield" of objects blindfolded.
3. Have others in the group guide them verbally through the minefield without touching them. Time each team.
4. The team who gets through the minefield the fastest, wins.
5. Make the point that some days working in a company can often feel like a "minefield"—stressful and difficult at times.
6. Tell the group that how we communicate with each other will help us all get through to the other side of difficult times.
7. Ask the team to rate the communication within the team on a scale of 1–10, with 10 being the highest. Ask volunteers to share and to give positive ideas on how to improve it.

Key Questions

- Why do you think communication is one of the most important elements of creating a healthy, productive work environment?
- What kinds of things must be communicated effectively within the team?

Key Points

- When communication is strong, service is excellent, associates are satisfied with their jobs, there is less conflict, and relationships are strong and fulfilling. When communication is weak, there is usually chaos, stress, and low service scores.
- Details on problems reported by customers are examples of things that must be communicated clearly if we are to improve service.
- We can communicate as a team through huddles, staff meetings, memos, customer feedback, and more.

Tips/Examples/Variations

Examples of good communication:

- Clear—Everyone needs to be on the same page and the message should be clear to all.
- Regular—It is daily, not only when problems arise.
- Equal—Everyone is responsible, not just leadership.

CATEGORY ▶ **COMMUNICATION**

Purpose: To practice asking questions and listening

Time Requirement: 10 minutes

Materials Needed: None

More often than not, a dissatisfied customer (internal or external) will not tell you where you went wrong. They will not approach you with a list of grievances or a summary of their experience. They will simply move on to another company or service a different department or team member. In order to ensure the best customer experience, it is important to ask open-ended questions and then genuinely listen. What are people *not* saying? The best way to solve that mystery is to put yourself in their shoes. This role-play exercise puts a creative spin on open-ended questions.

Directions

1. Select a leader and have them choose a famous person in history without revealing them to the group.
2. Allow each person to ask one yes or no question of the leader to uncover their identity.
3. The leader must only respond in yes or no answers.
4. The person who guesses the leader's identity wins.
5. Challenge each team member to choose an open-ended question and ask that question of at least one customer today. Use the information you learned to deliver excellent service.
6. Express to the team that your door is always open to listen to them.

Key Questions

- How important is listening to our customers?
- How does it make us feel when we are not listened to by another person?
- What are some open-ended questions that we can ask our customers to find out about their experience with our company?
- When you ask a customer if they were satisfied with the service and they respond "fine" in a flat tone of voice, what could they really be saying?

Key Points

- If we listen, our customers will tell us what we need to know to get them to continue choosing us.
- "Tell me something we could do to be of further assistance to you." And "Is there anything we could have done better?" are examples of open-ended questions we can use to show our customers we care.
- Great service involves listening, understanding, and responding to customers.
- It's important to listen for the things your customers aren't saying to you. Be curious.

Tips/Examples/Variations

Active listening skills include:

- Nodding your head.
- Saying things like "I see what you mean," or "I understand."
- Looking the other person in the eye.
- Not interrupting.
- Stopping whatever you are doing to show that you are paying attention.
- Repeating key points back to show that you understand the behaviors listed.

Purpose: To define what "Communicates Connections" means

Time Requirement: 10 minutes

Materials Needed: Flipchart or whiteboard; markers

I t can be difficult to see beyond our own desk. This has its drawbacks. If our work becomes disconnected from the whole, it might feel like busywork. This creates problems surrounding motivation. *Why is it so important that I get this report done right now, anyway?* To avoid this, there must be clear communication about the company as a whole. Individuals have to see the role they play in the greater scheme of the company's success. This can only be done through conversation. How committed are people to the company's mission statement? Does it resonate with them personally? People need to know the profound impact that they have on the entire company.

Directions

1. Ask the group what they think "Communicates Connections" means.
2. Ask why communicating how we are connected with the organization as a whole is important. Ask for ideas on how we can do that.
3. Facilitate the discussion by using the **Key Questions** and **Key Points** that follow.

Key Questions

- How can we stay connected with the mission of our company?
- What happens if we lose that connection?

Key Points

- "Communicates Connections" means to clearly communicate priorities and goals, share the long-term vision, and point out how each job is connected to the success of this organization.

Tips/Examples/Variations

Examples of how to communicate connections with the organization as a whole:

- Become familiar with the company's mission and value statements.
- Discuss with your team members and managers how your job is connected with the larger whole.
- Ask for feedback on how you can ensure that your work is helping the company at large.

Purpose: To discuss the meaning of "communicate first"

Time Requirement: 15 minutes

Materials Needed: Flipchart or whiteboard; markers

There are countless sayings about being proactive. "The early bird gets the worm" comes to mind. The same is true in regard to communication. Leaders are proactive in their communications with customers. Have you ever been in an establishment and didn't have to flag someone down to be helped? It is a great feeling and, more likely than not, you left that experience with a favorable view of the company. We "communicate first" verbally and nonverbally. Being proactive with both of these aspects of communication puts your team ahead of the competition and will support internal efforts within your organization.

Directions

1. Introduce the topic by saying that leaders speak first—whether it is being the first to greet a customer or to offer assistance to a team member. Say that "communicating first" means being proactive and taking initiative.
2. Ask the group what taking initiative and being proactive means.
3. Say that "communicating first" involves both nonverbal and verbal behavior. (Make two columns on the flipchart/whiteboard— label one "Nonverbal" and the other "Verbal.")
4. Ask the group for examples of nonverbal ways to "communicate first."
5. Ask the group for examples of verbal ways to "communicate first" (use the **Key Questions** and **Key Points** that follow to facilitate discussion).

6. Summarize the activity by saying that taking the initiative to "communicate first" shows that you care and that you are here to help.

Key Questions

- What does "communicate first" mean to you?
- Why is "communicating first" important?
- What is verbal behavior? What is nonverbal behavior?
- What are ways we can "communicate first"?
- What can happen if you don't "communicate first"?

Key Points

- "Communicating first" means using "conversation starters" to build relationships.
- "Communicating first" means being approachable so customers and team members can come to you.
- "Communicating first" can include greeting a customer first, wishing them a good day, and/or offering assistance.
- Verbal ways to "communicate first" include saying hello, using the individual's name, or acknowledging what you see or hear.
- Nonverbal behavior includes smiling, nodding, using eye contact, anticipating your team members' needs, and using open body language.
- By "communicating first," you demonstrate the signs of a "can-do" attitude.

CATEGORY ▶ COMMUNICATION

Purpose: To discuss why it is important to communicate first within our team

Time Requirement: 10 minutes

Materials Needed: None

It can be easy to assume that everyone is on the same page. However, policy changes and project directions can shift without certain employees ever getting the memo. This kind of miscommunication causes a disruption in workflow. Not only are these situations confusing and frustrating, but they result in productivity dips. How much time was lost arguing over policies or correcting mistakes? It is important to reemphasize the importance of internal communication by breaking down information barriers. Companies have to operate as teams, and teams only function if everyone has access to the same information. The playing field must be level and the machine well oiled.

Directions

1. Introduce the topic by asking the group to think about a time when a process or policy changed and it wasn't communicated before it happened. Ask them to share examples honestly (without fear of repercussion).
2. Ask them what resulted due to that lack of communication.
3. Ask the group how communication early on could have helped in this situation.
4. Discuss why there can be a lack of communication before a new process or policy is introduced. Ask how we might remove these barriers and use communication first.
5. Facilitate and debrief the discussion by using the **Key Questions** and **Key Points** that follow.

Key Questions

- When has there been a lack of communication at work?
- How did that impact your job?
- Why do you think there was a lack of communication?
- What are ways we can "communicate first" in order to avoid problems in the future?

Key Points

- We are often so busy in our daily activities that we forget to communicate information to each other.
- Lack of communication can cause major problems and frustration.
- Remember to take the time to communicate first to avoid challenges later. It can be as simple as an email, memo, or voice message.
- How does it make a customer feel when they get the "I don't know" look?

Tips/Examples/Variations

Examples of process or policy changes:

- Change in timesheet procedures.
- Change in sick day policies.
- Change in a computer procedure.

CATEGORY ► COMMUNICATION

Purpose: To ensure that connections are communicated effectively

Time Requirement: 10 minutes

Materials Needed: Flipchart or whiteboard; markers

Managers are the connection between specific teams and the larger company. It is the manager's responsibility to ensure that employees understand how their work plays into the company as a whole and helps further the goals of the entire group. As a result, a manager's communication skills are of paramount importance to the entire team. In order to best serve your team, open a conversation about what types of communication resonate with them. What do they need clarification on? The following activity provides a space for conversations that will help your associates tie their work to the mission and vision of the organization.

Directions

1. Ask the group what can happen if they lose the connection between what they are doing and how it impacts the customers and the organization as a whole.
2. Say that it is important that connections between their work and the company's vision are communicated clearly.
3. Ask the group for ideas on how you as their manager could be clearer about communicating these connections. Record their ideas.
4. Tell the group that you will use their ideas to ensure that a connection is made between their jobs and the value they provide the organization as a whole.

Key Questions

- How can I be clearer in communicating the value of your work to the organization?

Key Points

- Clear communication about the connection between our jobs and the mission of the company is critical.

Tips/Examples/Variations

Examples as to how a manager could be clearer about communicating connections:

- Announce and discuss any important company or policy changes as soon as you know them.
- Make the connection for team members by saying things like, "How you handled that customer is one of the reasons we have the reputation we do."

Purpose: To articulate the vision/mission of the organization

Time Requirement: 15 minutes

Materials Needed: None

It is important to know the vision and mission of our company. The company's vision informs all of the work that we do. Moreover, if we cannot articulate the company's vision, how can we expect to clarify that vision to customers? A company mission is a goal, and teams only function if they are striving toward the same, unified goal. We might all have different roles to play, but ultimately, those roles all help build components of a unified vision. The following activity creates a space to discuss the company vision and mission and how it might relate to the work we do on a daily basis.

Directions

1. Ask the group why it is important to be able to articulate the vision/mission of the organization.
2. Ask for ideas on what the vision/mission is. Supplement the information where needed.
3. Say that we're going to do a role-play between a new employee and a manager. Ask for two volunteers and assign who will be the new employee and who will be the manager.
4. Say that the pair is to imagine they are in a job interview and the new employee asks, "What is the vision of the company?" or "What is the mission of the company?" The manager should then respond to the question. The rest of the group is allowed to "coach" the manager.

5. Have the pair try it out. Then have a new pair try it out if they'd like.

6. Facilitate and debrief the discussion by using the **Key Questions** and **Key Points** that follow.

Key Questions

- What is the vision and mission of the company?
- Why should we be able to articulate it?

Key Points

- If we do not understand the vision or can't articulate it, it will be difficult to do our jobs and communicate this information to our customers.

Tips/Examples/Variations

- Bring in documents showing the company mission and value statements. Team members can work off of that for the role-play, if necessary.

CATEGORY ► COMMUNICATION

Purpose: To practice giving good instructions or directions

Time Requirement: 10 minutes

Materials Needed: None

Clarity with instructions requires being thorough. Oftentimes, we assume that the people we are communicating with share the same level of knowledge that we do on any given topic. However, this is usually not the case. It is widely understood that customers may need a thorough explanation, as they might not be as familiar with a topic as you are, but the same goes for team members. Teams are diverse and employees have varying roles, skill sets, and topical literacies. How can we ensure that our directions and instructions are clear? It is important to close the information gap in order to avoid miscommunication.

Directions

1. Ask the group why it is important to offer instructions or directions to a customer or team member.
2. Say we often assume customers or team members know how to do something or how to get to a certain location.
3. Ask the group how we can ensure that our directions or instructions are clear.
4. Facilitate the discussion by using the **Key Questions** and **Key Points** that follow.
5. Ask the group to practice giving clear instructions or directions today.

Key Questions

- Why is it important to offer help with directions?
- How can we be sure our directions are clear?
- What can happen if our instructions or directions are unclear?

Key Points

- Offering instructions or directions shows that you are going the extra mile with the customer or team member.
- Often, we assume people know how to do things or how to get somewhere.
- Make sure your instructions or directions are clear—ask the customer or team member to repeat back what you've said, or you repeat if necessary. Try to use simple terms and body language to aid in understanding (such as pointing).
- Unclear directions or instructions cause frustration, a lack of trust, and more time than necessary.
- Practice with other teammates giving directions to popular requested locations.

Tips/Examples/Variations

- An option is to identify the most commonly requested directions and have them practice giving those; for example, to the nearest ATM, to a company, to the nearest drugstore, and so on.

CHAPTER 3

DEVELOPING YOUR TALENT

CATEGORY ► **TALENT DEVELOPMENT**

Purpose: To teach participants how to develop clear and achievable goals

Time Requirement: 15 minutes

Materials Needed: Flipchart or whiteboard; markers

Specific, Measurable, Achievable, Result-Oriented, Time-Bound: **SMART.** When we set goals, we have to keep all of these aspects in mind. Specificity is integral to ensuring that we know what we are aiming at. Flying blindly toward goals often results in a fizzling out of the project. In a similar way, the goal must be measurable so that the team knows when the goal has been met. Is the goal within our grasp, realistic, attainable, achievable? Is the goal result-oriented? When we say result-oriented, we mean: Why this goal? What is to be gained? Finally, time-bound. There must be a set timeline to help guide progression toward a goal. These aspects go a long way in ensuring that goals are approached in an organized manner, helping optimize success.

Directions

1. Introduce the topic by stating that one of the best ways to achieve your goals is to make sure that the goals are **SMART**

(**Specific**, **Measurable**, **Achievable**, **Results-Oriented**, and **Time-Bound**).

2. Write SMART at the top of the flipchart or whiteboard.
3. Walk the participants through the SMART model by using the goal of "losing weight."
4. Ask the participants how measurable and specific this is (it is very general).
5. State that a way to make this goal more achievable is to break it down into the SMART components:
    a. Specific and Measurable: Lose 10 pounds and two inches on my waist.
    b. Achievable: By walking two miles every day.
    c. Results-Oriented: To feel more comfortable in my clothes.
    d. Time-Bound: By (Month) (Day), (Year).
6. Have each participant identify a goal or solution to a problem they are facing.
7. Have them use the SMART model to make the goal more specific, measurable, and time-bound.

Key Questions

- Is the goal achievable?
- Have you included a time frame?
- How does the SMART model increase the likelihood that the goal/solution will be met and implemented?

Key Points

- Goals are more likely to be reached if they follow the SMART model.

Tips/Examples/Variations

Another Example:

- S and M: Attend one computer training class on Excel.
- A: By the end of 2022.
- R: In order to create my budgets more quickly and easily.
- T: So I can submit my new budget by January 2023.

CATEGORY ► TALENT DEVELOPMENT

Purpose: To continue to build and capitalize on individual strengths

Time Requirement: 10 minutes

Materials Needed: Flipchart or whiteboard; markers; paper and pens

A team only works because the individuals that comprise it possess unique skill sets and talents. These talents, when put together, help the team progress toward goals while covering each other's weaknesses. As such, it is important to develop these individual talents. It all starts with recognizing that talent. Open a discussion about the strengths of individuals on your team. How can those strengths be further developed and honed? Focusing on strengths is a key to success. Focusing on our weaknesses is a path to failure. Subsequently, putting stock in your team's strengths is a valuable use of time. It is not common, but some members of the team might not be aware of their own strengths. In the event this occurs, have another team member point out one of their strengths for them. We have to recognize our talents in order to employ them.

Directions

1. Ask for each team member to share something they do really well in their job. (It is likely that this topic has been discussed before so they will have something in mind. If not, have a team member point out a strength.)
2. Ask why it is important to keep building on our strengths. Ask what happens if we don't.

3. Ask the team to think of ways that they can continue to build on one of their strengths.

4. Ask for volunteers to share their ideas.

Key Questions

- Why is it important to continue to focus on our strengths?
- What happens if we don't?
- How can we further build our strengths?

Key Points

- Studies show that focusing on a few of our greatest strengths, rather than our weaknesses, is a key to success.
- If we don't focus on our strengths, we lose confidence and can lose our skill in that area.

Tips/Examples/Variations

Examples as to how we can build on our strengths:

- Learn new ways to use our strengths.
- Practice them.
- Read about them or attend training classes.
- Teach another team member your special skills.

CATEGORY ► **TALENT DEVELOPMENT**

Purpose: To practice giving feedback effectively

Time Requirement: 15 minutes

Materials Needed: Flipchart or whiteboard; markers

Feedback is a productive way to better the team. However, feedback is not always helpful when framed the wrong way. Have you ever received feedback that was not constructive? It likely made you feel a bit frustrated. Feedback that is unhelpful is ultimately more damaging than beneficial. Oftentimes, the person offering unhelpful feedback has no intention of being destructive. While their heart could be in the right place, though, the reception is what matters. This activity helps distinguish quality feedback from unhelpful feedback. It also opens up a space to explain what types of feedback resonate with your team.

Directions

1. Ask the group to think about when they received feedback that was unhelpful or made them angry.
2. Make two columns on the flipchart: "Helpful" and "Not Helpful."
3. Ask them what specifically made the feedback not helpful. Record their answers on the flipchart under "Not Helpful."
4. Say that many people are not good at giving feedback—it's a hard thing to do.
5. Ask the group to think of ways that would make feedback more helpful. Use the **Key Points** that follow to supplement the discussion. Record their responses under "Helpful."
6. Break the group into pairs. Tell them that they will take turns giving each other feedback using the ideas listed under "Helpful."

7. Have them role-play a scenario between two team members. One team member is giving the other feedback regarding pitching in when the other gets busy.

8. Debrief the activity by using the **Key Questions** that follow.

Key Questions

- How did it go? Were you receptive to the feedback? If not, why?
- What did your partner do well?
- What suggestions would you give your partner?

Key Points

Use these tips to give feedback effectively:

- Be clear and specific—define exactly what the problem is.
- Focus on the positive and how solving the problem would benefit all.
- Focus on the behavior, not the person—for example, "When the trash isn't taken out, the kitchen starts to stink," not "You never take out the garbage!"
- Avoid saying "you"—use "I" statements instead.
- Offer to help.
- Be open to feedback yourself.

Tips/Examples/Variations

- A tip for role-play: Helpful feedback might include asking how one could help, offering to pitch in, asking the team member what they think would help.

CATEGORY ▶ TALENT DEVELOPMENT

Purpose: To examine the benefits of being an everyday learner

Time Requirement: 10 minutes

Materials Needed: A beach ball with questions about the company written in permanent marker (see example questions below)

Learning is a skill and as such it must be exercised. There are a multitude of reasons that people neglect to work that muscle. Sometimes they are afraid, other times they are apathetic or lazy. Actively learning, being inquisitive, is difficult, which is why additional effort and emphasis must be placed on that skill. We should constantly be improving and learning. The workplace is not just a job, but a place to grow. How often are we learning from our environment and our fellow team members? Being an active learner is critical to our success—not just in the company, but as people. We should be stronger and more skilled today than we were yesterday.

Directions

1. In a circle, toss the ball to team members and have them answer a question they choose on the ball.
2. Use the answers as discussion on these important facts about your company.
3. Ask the group if anyone learned anything new.
4. Debrief with **Key Questions** and **Key Points**.

Key Questions
- What stops us from being a learner? Fear, laziness, being busy with tasks, apathy, and so on.
- When was the last time you were asked to learn something new from a manager or fellow team member?

Key Points
- Being a learner is critical to our success.
- Asking questions is a great way to learn.
- People (such as parents, teachers, and managers) can help us learn, but ultimately learning is up to us.
- If we want to move forward in life and work, we need to take responsibility for our own learning.

Tips/Examples/Variations
Example questions:
- When was the company founded?
- What tools can be used to learn how our customers feel about the company?
- What produces the most revenue for our company?

CATEGORY ▶ **TALENT DEVELOPMENT**

Purpose: To develop fresh ways to measure our department's performance

Time Requirement: 10 minutes

Materials Needed: Flipchart or whiteboard; markers

Growth appears in many different forms, which can make it difficult to track. Many companies track growth through evaluations and other means. However, evaluations are often too rigid and devolve growth into a series of numbers. How can we accurately track the growth of our talent? In order to improve performance, we have to actively be searching for new ways to grow. The following activity allows employees the opportunity to discuss growth and encourages them to take responsibility for their development, which improves motivation and dedication to the team as a whole.

Directions

1. Explain to the group that we are always looking for ways to improve our performance.
2. Ask: "How do we know if we are growing?"
3. Divide the group into two teams.
4. Instruct each team to brainstorm some new and fun ways that we can engage one another to facilitate and measure growth within our company.
5. Bring the team back together to discuss their ideas and debrief using **Key Questions** and **Key Points** that follow.

Key Questions

- How do we currently measure performance in our company?
- How do we measure our individual contribution to the team?
- How do you take responsibility for your growth?
- What resources do you leverage to support your growth?
- What areas could you personally work on and improve to benefit the overall performance of your department?
- How can we make growth and skill development a team activity?

Key Points

- As individual team members in a department, we all have a vital role to play. Our collective success depends on each one of us playing a part and giving our personal best.
- To do our best, we must take personal responsibility for our growth and ownership of our role in the success of our company.
- Developing our talents and skills takes effort, but together we can leverage our successes to fuel our drive and motivation to improve our performance.

Tips/Examples/Variations

- Challenge each department to come up with an internal, team-led system for tracking progress on improving customer feedback. Present an award to the most innovative team.

CATEGORY ▶ TALENT DEVELOPMENT

Purpose: To practice letting go of our limitations

Time Requirement: 10 minutes

Materials Needed: Paper; pens

If you think you can't, you won't. The limits we place on ourselves have a habit of becoming self-fulfilling prophecies. Our mindset has a massive impact on our growth. Surprisingly, the barrier to our success is often ourselves. So how are we limiting ourselves from trying new things or developing our skills? It is important to identify areas in which we may be holding ourselves back. Only then can we push ourselves out of our comfort zones. Growth involves risk—one cannot be present without the other. It is important to open up a discussion about the "growing pains" we might be avoiding so that we can better push ourselves to confront them.

Directions

1. Give each participant a sheet of paper and a pen.
2. Explain to the group that we all have limiting beliefs that keep us from trying new things, developing our skills, and reaching our potential both on and off the job (see next page for examples).
3. Ask each participant to write down some examples of limiting beliefs or ideas they have about themselves or their capabilities that keep them from being their personal best.
4. Debrief using **Key Questions** and **Key Points** that follow.

Key Questions

- How do our beliefs about ourselves hold us back from doing our best?
- Why is it important to question our self-imposed limitations?
- How can we take risks by testing our limitations?
- How do limiting beliefs about ourselves limit our growth and development?

Key Points

- When we tell ourselves we can't do something, we are less willing to try.
- When we tell ourselves we can't, we create a self-fulfilling prophecy whether it's true or not.
- If we fail to challenge ourselves and try, we will surely fail to grow.

Tips/Examples/Variations

Examples of limiting beliefs:

- I'm not good at math.
- I'm not going back to school because I'm not a good test taker.
- I'm not smart enough to ever do that task as well as Joe.
- They will never give me a chance to be manager, so why bother trying?

CATEGORY ► **TALENT DEVELOPMENT**

Purpose: To identify one area of development

Time Requirement: 10 minutes

Materials Needed: None

The why and the where are fundamental aspects of job development. First, the team needs to understand why it is important to keep developing our skills and evolving the way we do our jobs. Constantly growing and developing helps us remain proactive, relevant, and efficient. Secondarily, we have to know where or what direction we are developing in. What areas would we like to see growth in? Before actual development can take place, the why and the where must be hashed out, which is what the following activity helps you accomplish.

Directions

1. Ask the team why it is important to keep developing our skills or improving the way we do our job.
2. Ask each team member to identify one area of development that they'd like to work on over the next month.
3. Ask for volunteers to share their responses.
4. Ask: "What will make it easier to work on this development area?" Discuss.
5. Debrief the activity by using the **Key Questions** and **Key Points** that follow.

Key Questions

- What resources can I use to work on my development area?
- Where do you want to be in five years?

- How do you see our industry changing over the next two to five years?
- What resources and training exist within the company that you can take advantage of?

Key Points

- Developing our skills and making improvements helps to keep us competitive.
- Most people graduating college will have to work for fifty years, meaning they must keep their skill set sharp for half a century.
- Companies are looking for people to increase their contribution over time.

Tips/Examples/Variations

Examples of areas of development:

- Practicing communicating more effectively with customers, such as speaking slowly and loudly and using fewer rather than more words.
- Practicing being more attentive to details and working more thoroughly.

CATEGORY ▶ **TALENT DEVELOPMENT**

Purpose: To practice continuous learning

Time Requirement: 10 minutes

Materials Needed: None

Learning keeps us from growing stagnant. If our work offers us no challenge and is undynamic, we lose our energy and excitement toward it. To counter this, we can push ourselves to learn new skills, approach our work differently, create added value, and constantly better our performance. This excitement radiates out, not only impacting company culture, but customers as well. The activity below allows employees to explore this concept through the lens of non-work-related activities or hobbies. What new things can we learn to increase job performance? How do we stay dynamic in the workplace?

Directions

1. Ask for volunteers to share one hobby that they are passionate about.
2. Ask the rest of the group to identify one of the hobbies mentioned that they'd like to learn.
3. Ask the group what it feels like to learn new things.
4. Discuss using the **Key Points** that follow.
5. Say that learning new things keeps us excited and energized. Learning new things on the job keeps our team productive.

Key Points

- Learning new things keeps us energized and excited.
- That excitement helps team morale and customer service.

Tips/Examples/Variations

Examples of continuous learning:

- Asking team members to share how they approach a task.
- Learning more about a particular skill necessary for your job.
- Job shadowing a team member whom you work with closely, but who has a job different from yours.
- Asking for feedback from your manager on ways to improve key job skills.

CATEGORY ▶ **TALENT DEVELOPMENT**

Purpose: To set one challenging goal this week

Time Requirement: 10 minutes

Materials Needed: None

Why do we challenge ourselves? What is the point in pushing ourselves outside our comfort zone? Without challenge, we never have the opportunity to grow and better ourselves. This is the point of stretch goals. Stretch goals are challenges, but not so far out of reach that chances of success are nil. Growth is incremental. Just as Rome was not built in a day, neither are new habits and skills. This activity allows employees to discuss what goals might be beneficial to their development as well as how they can achieve those goals in a challenging, yet appropriate manner.

Directions
1. Ask why we want to set goals that are challenging for us.
2. Say that you'd like each team member to set one challenging goal in their job role to accomplish this week.
3. Say that "challenging" means enough so it's a bit of a stretch, but not so much that it is unrealistic.
4. Break the group into pairs and have them share their goals.
5. Debrief by using the **Key Question** and **Key Point** that follow.

Key Questions
• Why do we want to have "stretch" goals?

Key Points

- Challenging goals motivate us and make us feel good about our capabilities.

Tips/Examples/Variations

- Encourage the team members to set a goal that is achievable, but more challenging than typical goals.

| CATEGORY ▶ TALENT DEVELOPMENT |

Purpose: To show we can stretch more than we think we can

Time Requirement: 10 minutes

Materials Needed: None

We are more capable than we think we are. It is human nature to constantly push our limits, to expand, and to push the boundaries. This mentality took us to the moon, cured diseases, and informs ever-increasing scores from Olympic athletes. Oftentimes, we assume that we have hit our limit, but we have much more in us. We seek comfort when we should become comfortable with the uncomfortable. The following exercise is a motivational one, designed to push employees to new heights and to break down mental barriers that say "I can't."

Directions

1. Ask for a volunteer. Have them come to the front of the room.
2. Tell them to stretch one arm as high as they can. Make a mark where their fingers end.
3. Ask for another volunteer. Have the person come up and do the same exercise but mark it in a new spot.
4. Now have each come up again. Say that you know they can stretch farther than their first try.
5. Have them try again. Encourage them by clapping and giving positive feedback such as "you can do it!" Invite the rest of the group to encourage as well.
6. See who can get farther than their first try.
7. Debrief the exercise by using the **Key Questions** and **Key Points** that follow.

Key Questions

- How can we stretch ourselves and our capabilities?
- Does positive feedback help motivate you to stretch yourself further?

Key Points

- We have a lot of potential; tap into it and encourage each other to stretch!
- Limits and boundaries are meant to be broken!
- Don't let yourself become your own barrier.

Tips/Examples/Variations

Examples of ways to stretch yourself at work:

- Challenge yourself to complete a task more thoroughly.
- Challenge yourself to learn something new to make your job easier.
- Take on a new project that encourages you to learn new skills.

CHAPTER 4

GENERATING INCLUSION

CATEGORY ► INCLUSION

Purpose: To define what "Develops Equitable Workplaces" means

Time Requirement: 15 minutes

Materials Needed: Flipchart or whiteboard; markers

Equitable workplaces are marked by having a spirit of inclusion, fairness, and respect. Teams succeed when these are present. Without them, people lose motivation and loyalty to the team. Nobody wants to give their effort and time to an environment that disrespects them. Inclusion, respect, and fairness are the stitches that hold together a strong company culture. Diversity is important and with it comes diversity of thought. That means more perspectives and creative solutions to the largest challenges your team faces. Don't just respect the differences in your team—value them.

Directions

1. Ask the group what they think "Develops Equitable Workplaces" means. Record their responses on the flipchart/whiteboard. Add the following if not mentioned:

      a. Develops a spirit of inclusion.

      b. Treats people fairly and equitably.

      c. Recognizes the values and differences in people.

      d. Shows respect for others.

2. Ask them how having an equitable workplace benefits us and the company.
3. Ask for ideas on how we can create a more equitable workplace.
4. Summarize by using the **Key Questions** and **Key Points** that follow.

Key Questions

- What does an "Equitable Workplace" mean?
- What are the benefits of having an equitable workplace?
- How can we create and maintain an equitable workplace?

Key Points

- An equitable workplace is one that has a spirit of inclusion, treats people fairly and respectfully, and recognizes the values and differences in people.
- If we believe we are being treated fairly and respectfully, we'll be happier and more productive in our jobs.
- It takes awareness and effort to maintain an equitable workplace. If you observe things that are not promoting fairness, speak to your manager and/or come up with ideas to make the workplace better.

Tips/Examples/Variations

Examples of benefits of equitable workplaces:

- More opportunity for everyone.
- A pleasant and welcoming place to work.
- Fair treatment for all.

CATEGORY ► **INCLUSION**

Purpose: To identify what we have in common

Time Requirement: 10 minutes

Materials Needed: Paper and pens

While people are unique, more often than not, many aspects of us are similar. We all walk through life with our own specific lenses through which we view the world—lenses informed by our own irreplicable life experiences. This creates diversity. But at our core, we are all more similar than we might initially recognize. Teams, at the very least, have one thing in common—their shared commitment to the company mission and overall team purpose. This exercise allows us to recognize the similarity—as well as the diversity—in our coworkers.

Directions

1. Ask the group to find a partner. If there's an uneven number, participate with the group.
2. Give them three minutes to identify how many things they have in common. Give them each a piece of paper and pen and tell them to record their findings.
3. Facilitate and summarize the exercise by using the **Key Questions** and **Key Points** that follow.

Key Questions

- How many of you found more than ten things in common?
- What unusual things did you learn about each other?
- How did you find out what you had in common?
- How does learning what we have in common help our team and workplace?

Key Points

- We often have more in common with each other than we think.
- We may have different backgrounds or experiences but share the same values, way of life, and so on.
- These commonalities can help our team move forward, especially in times of change or conflict.

Tips/Examples/Variations

- A variation of this is to have each person stand up with a piece of paper and a pen and go around the room with as many people as needed to come up with five things they have in common with other people in the room.

CATEGORY ► **INCLUSION**

Purpose: To identify ways to resolve team conflicts

Time Requirement: 15 minutes

Materials Needed: Flipchart or whiteboard; markers

When working in a group capacity, people are bound to disagree with one another at some point. There is not anything inherently wrong with disagreement—in fact, it can prompt fruitful discussions about the direction of a project. However, when these discussions escalate into arguments, they become conflict. Team conflict is incredibly detrimental to morale. When the team fights, communication breaks down and motivation drops. Unlike most discussions, conflicts are unproductive. Therefore, it is wise to have a few rules of engagement to help de-escalate contentious situations. The following activity introduces a five-step conflict resolution strategy, which can be the difference between discussion and conflict.

Directions

1. Ask the group how team conflict can be detrimental.
2. Say that resolving conflict can help us move forward and have better morale.
3. Say that there's a five-step way to resolve conflict (write this on the flipchart/whiteboard):
   a. Set ground rules.
   b. Listen.
   c. Find areas of agreement.
   d. Brainstorm solutions.
   e. Reach an agreement.
4. Ask for a volunteer to share an example of when he or she has faced conflict.

5. Ask the volunteer if he or she used any of these steps. Use that example to walk through the steps (the steps are detailed in the **Key Points** that follow).

6. Debrief using the **Key Questions** that follow.

Key Questions

- What does "set ground rules" mean?
- What are ways to show we're listening?
- What does "find areas of agreement" mean?
- How is brainstorming solutions together helpful?
- How can we reach an agreement together?

Key Points

- ***Set ground rules.*** Agree to work together and set rules such as no name-calling, blaming, yelling, or interrupting.
- ***Listen.*** Let each person describe his or her point of view without interruption. The point is to understand what a person wants and why they want it.
- ***Find areas of agreement.*** Establish facts and issues that everyone can agree on and determine what is important to each person.
- ***Brainstorming.*** List all options without judging them or feeling that they must be carried out. Try to think of solutions where everyone gains something.
- ***Reach an agreement.*** Each person should state his or her interpretation of the agreement. Try writing the agreement down and checking back at a later time to see how it is working.
- ***This same learning can be applied to problem resolution with customers.*** The agreement is not always the remedy—it may in fact just put a bandage over the deeper conflict.

Tips/Examples/Variations

- A variation of this would be to have them practice the five steps. Once you review them, break the group into pairs and give them a scenario (the conflict could be over workspace, time off, etc.). They could then practice the five steps in that scenario.

CATEGORY ► INCLUSION

Purpose: To develop appreciation for differences of opinion

Time Requirement: 15 minutes

Materials Needed: Picture from a magazine that shows people engaged in some sort of activity or interaction—no words

We all see things differently. The unique perspectives of individuals can be understood as glasses. Everyone has their own special pair. The lenses of these glasses are informed by our own life experiences, biases, skills, and passions. Because of this, many people can interpret a situation differently, despite processing the same information. It is important to understand this fundamental concept of human nature when working in teams. The activity below allows employees to explore this concept in a tangible way, opening a conversation about perspective.

Directions

1. Hold up the picture for the participants to see; pass it around if necessary.
2. Post it on the wall or a flipchart.
3. Ask for volunteers to share their interpretation of what is happening in the picture (use the **Key Questions** that follow).
4. Share the true situation and outcome of the picture with the group (from the captions that you've cut off or the news story).
5. State that it's not important who described the picture correctly, but how we came to our interpretations.
6. Discuss how we can have differences of opinion, which all share some truth.

7. Ask the group how this relates to their workplace. Have we ever discounted someone's opinion? What is the impact of doing that? What would happen if we made an effort to see the "other side of the story"? How would that improve our jobs/workplace?

Key Questions

- What is being said?
- How do these people feel?
- What are their motivations?
- What caused the situation?
- What might be an outcome?
- What are you using to make these interpretations? (Noticing their body language, facial expressions, and the location, etc.)

Key Points

- Appreciating differences of opinion helps team members feel valued and part of a team.
- Understanding and accepting differences of opinion may help us approach challenges more effectively and solve problems more quickly.

Tips/Examples/Variations

- Pick a picture that has a lot going on and could be interpreted in many different ways.

Purpose: To identify ways to show respect for one another

Time Requirement: 10 minutes

Materials Needed: Flipchart or whiteboard; markers; paper and pens

Respect. It is integral to a healthy workplace culture. Communication and motivation hinge on respect. Conversations about company vision or team projects cannot be held without mutual respect from all parties involved. When teams do not respect one another and do not view their counterparts as equals, ideas are not truly heard and arguments may break out. This, in turn, drastically impacts motivation. How is respect cultivated? It all starts with a conversation. This activity provides employees with an opportunity to express what respect means to them, allowing the company to move forward in a respectful manner toward success.

Directions

1. Introduce the topic by asking why it is important to respect our team members.
2. Ask what benefits we (team and organization) gain from respecting each other.
3. Break the group into pairs and ask them to come up with ways to show respect for each of the letters: $R - E - S - P - E - C - T$. Give each pair a piece of paper on which to record their answers.
4. After five minutes, ask the group to share what they came up with.
5. Instruct the group to use one of the examples they came up with on the job this week.

Key Questions

- Why is respect in the workplace important?
- How does it benefit us? Our customers?
- What are ways we can show respect for each other?

Key Points

- Respecting each other is the heart and soul of a good team and work environment.
- There are many ways to demonstrate respect to our team members.

Tips/Examples/Variations

A variation is to do this activity with the whole group, instead of pairs. This would save time if needed. Example:

- **R**—Remind a teammate about what a good job they are doing.
- **E**—Educate other team members on things that might help them on the job.
- **S**—Show empathy when a team member has a difficult day.
- **P**—Practice attentive listening to show you care about what others have to say.
- **E**—End each day by saying "have a good night" to your team members.
- **C**—Display caring and pay attention to what my teammate has to say.
- **T**—Try to keep an open mind when someone has an opinion different from yours.

CATEGORY ► **INCLUSION**

Purpose: To uncover grievances that are getting in the way of an equitable and productive workplace

Time Requirement: 15 minutes

Materials Needed: Drawing of a large tree on a flipchart or whiteboard; cutouts of red apples, yellow pears, and oranges—enough so each participant could have three of each—the cutouts should be three to four inches in diameter; flipchart or whiteboard; markers; tape

In order for a team to function, they must have an avenue to air their grievances. When people do not feel comfortable expressing challenges they are facing, those challenges have a tendency to pile up and eventually explode. Suppressed thoughts and feelings resurface with a vengeance. For this reason, it is important that employees feel comfortable speaking up about the challenges they are facing in the workplace. This activity opens up an avenue for that communication and, if reinforced, will maintain the space for open communication down the line.

Directions

1. Divide the group into smaller teams of two to four people.
2. Give each team a few pieces of each "fruit."
3. Ask the group to discuss among their team the challenges and/or grievances they have regarding their workplace.
4. Say that the apples represent crucial challenges, the oranges represent significant challenges, and the pears represent minor challenges.

5. Tell the group to record their challenges on the appropriate piece of fruit—three total.
6. Have the teams place their fruit on the tree using tape.
7. Read the challenges out loud and get the group's input on how to prioritize them.
8. Let the group know how you plan to address their challenges/ grievances.

Key Questions

- What challenges are getting in the way of this team performing better?
- What grievances do you have that, if addressed, would make your work life easier? What challenges listed here are things you can help me address?

Key Points

- An equitable workplace is one where grievances can be aired without judgment or retaliation.
- An equitable workplace allows open communication.
- An equitable workplace addresses barriers to team unity and productivity.

Tips/Examples/Variations

- A variation to save time would be for them to use just one piece of fruit to indicate their challenge or grievance.

CATEGORY ► **INCLUSION**

Purpose: To practice empathy within the team

Time Requirement: 10 minutes

Materials Needed: Paper and pens

Proper communication and respect requires a great deal of empathy. Believe it or not, empathy is a muscle that can be worked. How can we learn to walk a mile in someone else's shoes? How can we see a situation from multiple perspectives? The activity below exercises our empathy muscles. Articulating the experiences of other people, despite not having personal encounters with those experiences, helps us better relate to others. This makes communication and mutual respect infinitely easier.

Directions

1. Give the definition of *empathy* and ensure that each team member understands the meaning.
2. Give a piece of paper and a pen to each participant.
3. Ask them to write down one fear they have—tell them not to write their name on the piece of paper. Collect the papers.
4. Have each person randomly select and read someone else's fear. After the person reads the fear, have him or her explain to the group how that person might feel.
5. Facilitate a discussion by using the **Key Questions** that follow. Include any **Key Points** they might have missed.

Key Questions

- What was it like to imagine the fear of another group member?
- What did we learn about each other?
- How does this exercise help us become more empathetic?
- Why is empathy an important part of an equitable workplace?

Key Points

- We all have different fears, values, and experiences.
- Reflecting on how another team member feels helps us fine-tune our empathy skills.
- Seeking out and understanding how another might feel helps us build a team environment that is accepting and compassionate.
- Be hospitable! It's our culture to be hospitable to customers and team members.

Tips/Examples/Variations

- Definition of *empathy*: One's ability to recognize, perceive, and feel the emotion of another.

CATEGORY ► INCLUSION

Purpose: To recognize a team member who has demonstrated fairness and respect

Time Requirement: 10 minutes

Materials Needed: A heart-shaped sticker, piece of candy, or paper cutout.

People can generally agree that a workplace should be fair, respectful, and equitable. However, people may have varying ideas of what that should look like. These different perceptions of "fairness" can lead to disagreements, or people feeling as though they are not treated with respect, even if that isn't the intention. In order to get everyone on the same page, an example must be provided. In the following exercise, team members are recognized for their commitment to office equity, while upholding a standard for the group. It all starts with one person and spreads from there.

Directions

1. Before the huddle, identify a team member who has been especially effective at demonstrating the principles of an equitable workplace—respect, openness, fairness, and empathy.
2. Introduce the topic by quickly reviewing the principles.
3. Say that one member of the team has especially demonstrated these principles effectively.
4. Award the team member the heart cutout or sticker.
5. Give the team member a round of applause.

Key Questions

- Why is an equitable workplace important?
- What are ways we can foster an equitable workplace?

Key Points

- An equitable workplace makes it more enjoyable to come to work and helps us do our jobs better.
- When we are happy at work, our customers benefit too!

Tips/Examples/Variations

- A variation is to award each team member a sticker or candy. Be specific in giving each team member feedback on how they've been effective at promoting an equitable workplace.

CATEGORY ► INCLUSION

Purpose: To demonstrate the importance of focusing on others

Time Requirement: 10 minutes

Materials Needed: None

In a world like ours, we often find ourselves running a mile a minute, just trying to stay afloat. This hectic pace of life promotes a very "me"-centric mindset. Can you think of the last time you held an exchange without using the word *I*? While there is nothing inherently wrong with focusing on ourselves from time to time, productive communication can only occur when we put attention on the other person. The following exercise highlights how "me"-centric our conversations tend to be. More importantly, it helps work our conversational muscles by forcing us to put our attention on our conversation partner.

Directions

1. Say that sometimes we forget to focus on others and instead focus on ourselves.
2. Ask the participants to find a partner.
3. Tell them to talk about anything they want. The one rule is that they CAN'T use the word *I*.
4. Time them for a minute or two and then tell them to switch partners and let the partner try.
5. Debrief the activity by using the **Key Questions** and **Key Points** that follow.

Key Questions

- How many of you were able to talk without using *I*?
- Why is it so difficult?
- What's it like to listen to someone who starts every sentence with *I*?
- How can we communicate better to focus on the other person?

Key Points

- It's refreshing to hear people talk about things other than themselves.
- It's hard to not use *I*, but it encourages us to focus on others.
- Focusing on others builds empathy and teamwork.
- Customers will see and feel the CAN-DO ATTITUDE throughout each department. We can all enjoy the positive results in the customer feedback.

Tips/Examples/Variations

- A variation is for you to pick a volunteer with you as the speaker to demonstrate avoiding *I*. You could then end the activity there or have them practice. Have fun with this!

CATEGORY ▶ INCLUSION

Purpose: To learn something new about another team member or employee or customer

Time Requirement: 10 minutes

Materials Needed: None

How well do we know our own team? Teams function best when we know the people working alongside us. This way, we more effectively find strategies that play to the team's strengths. How do your coworkers best communicate? How do they like to be recognized? What are their strong suits? Success is a team effort, and teams do not function without mutual understanding and cooperation. The following exercise creates a space for individuals to reach out to their team. Through this, they may learn something new or form a friendship. No matter the outcome, the team will be stronger for it.

Directions

1. Ask the group why it is helpful to reach out and learn things about our team members.
2. Tell the group that their task today is to find one person (preferably one they don't know as well as others) and to ask them to share one thing that they might not know about them. Say that the purpose of doing this is for us to get to know each other.
3. Tell the group that they, too, should share one thing that the other employee may not know about them.
4. Tell them to stay away from sharing things that are too personal.

Key Questions

- Why is it helpful to get to know our team members?
- How does it make us feel when people reach out to us?
- How can we learn new things about our customers?
- How can we use that customer insight to increase loyalty?

Key Points

- Learning about each other allows us to appreciate our differences and our commonalities.
- Appreciating differences is an important step in developing an equitable workplace.
- Pay attention to the customers' interests—magazines they enjoy, food or beverages they purchase, exercise routines, and so on.
- Acting on the customer-specific insight will demonstrate our commitment to outrageously pleasing our customers.

Tips/Examples/Variations

Questions that team members could ask each other:

- What's your favorite hobby? Restaurant?
- What do you like most about your job?
- What special skills do you have?

CATEGORY ▶ **INCLUSION**

Purpose: To practice addressing conflict on the team

Time Requirement: 10 minutes

Materials Needed: None

When conflict occurs within a team setting, the team breaks down. Morale is lost, as coworkers lose motivation, having just spent their energy on a conflict. Productivity is lowered as a result. Communication halts as coworkers stop sharing information in an attempt to avoid another conflict. Trust is broken. However, conflict is bound to happen. Instead of ignoring it and letting it fester, it is best to address it head-on and in the moment. The goal isn't to win a conflict, but to de-escalate it. Moreover, it is important to assess whether or not stepping into a conflict would be productive. Would my addition to this discussion de-escalate the issue or add fuel to the fire? The following activity creates a space to discuss conflict management.

Directions

1. Ask the group how conflict on the team causes us to lose morale and be less productive in our work.
2. Say that we want to address conflict when it exists.
3. Ask the group for ideas on how team members could address conflict between other team members.
4. Say that there are times when we might not want to step in. Ask the group in what circumstances we would want to stay out of a conflict or bring it to someone else to handle.
5. Encourage the group to take the initiative to address conflict on the team, if appropriate.

Key Questions

- How can conflict on the team cause us to lose morale and be less productive?
- When do we want to address the conflict?
- When do we want to stay out of it and notify our supervisor?
- What are some benefits to addressing the conflict?
- What are some consequences of not addressing the conflict?

Key Points

- Conflict among team members causes unnecessary stress for the team.
- Conflict may cause us to be less productive.
- If there's conflict on the team, it can branch out to other teams and to our customers.

Tips/Examples/Variations

Examples of when we might not want to step in to a conflict:

- When it is a long-standing conflict that has been addressed before.
- When it is a conflict that is very personal or is based on widely different personalities or values.

CATEGORY ► INCLUSION

Purpose: To practice giving a team member or customer the benefit of the doubt

Time Requirement: 10 minutes

Materials Needed: Flipchart or whiteboard; markers; paper and pens

A major aspect of inclusion is understanding. Understanding, or giving people the benefit of the doubt, assumes the best intentions until proven otherwise. More often than not, when conflict occurs, it isn't because a team member is actively trying to sabotage the group. The intentions behind actions are usually positive, but the outcome is muddied by miscommunication and other factors. Assigning blame and assuming the worst intentions in someone only adds fuel to the fire. Instead, we should act as though people are innocent until proven guilty. This grace is a form of mutual respect and a norm of successful teams and organizations.

Directions

1. Review what "give the benefit of the doubt" means.
2. Say that giving the benefit of the doubt means believing in the good of someone, rather than the bad.
3. Tell the group you'd like them to find one opportunity in the next few days to give someone the benefit of the doubt.
4. Ask the group for examples of situations when you might do this.
5. Use the **Key Questions** and **Key Points** that follow to facilitate discussion.

Key Questions

- What does "give the benefit of the doubt" mean?
- Why do we want to do that with each other and our customers?
- What are some situations where we could do that?

Key Points

- "Give the benefit of the doubt" means believing in the good of someone, instead of the bad.
- Giving the benefit of the doubt shows we trust and believe in each other.

Tips/Examples/Variations

Examples of situations in which we could give the benefit of the doubt are:

- When a team member is late, not assuming they intended to be late but assuming they got stuck in traffic, had problems at home, and so on.
- Saying "good morning" to a team member rather than "Why were you late? You are always late!"
- Saying to a customer "I will be happy to help you" rather than "I don't have a record that you reserved a room."

CATEGORY ► **INCLUSION**

Purpose: To enhance teamwork by getting to know each other

Time Requirement: 10 minutes

Materials Needed: Flipchart or whiteboard; markers

How can we learn about our coworkers? Knowing who you are working with is integral to team success. Conversation comes easily to some people, while others tend to be more introverted. Because of this, it can be beneficial to open a space to discuss getting to know one another. Traditional icebreakers can feel patronizing and unproductive. Instead of directing people to share a set of information in the form of an icebreaker, the following activity provides a structure for employees to ask the questions, and subsequently learn, about the aspects of their coworkers they are genuinely curious about.

Directions

1. Say: In order for the team to work most effectively together, it helps to know a little more about each other.
2. Ask the group to brainstorm a list of questions they'd like to know about each other. Tell them to stay away from questions that are too personal.
3. Review the list and narrow it down to two or three questions (eliminate any questions that are too personal or inappropriate).
4. Have a few volunteers answer the three questions.
5. Summarize by asking how we can continue to learn about each other.

Key Questions

- How does knowing a little bit more about each other help with teamwork?
- How can we continue to learn about each other?

Key Points

- Sometimes we are so busy with work that we don't take the time to get to know our team.
- Each of us brings unique experiences and interests to the team, which helps us function better.

Tips/Examples/Variations

Sample questions:

- Do you have pets?
- What's your favorite movie?
- What famous person would you like to have dinner with if you had the chance?

CHAPTER 5

BUILDING TEAM HARMONY

CATEGORY ► TEAM BUILDING

Purpose: To acknowledge fellow employees

Time Requirement: 10 minutes

Materials Needed: None

Recognition is the fuel on the motivational fire. When individuals do not feel like their work is appreciated, they find themselves searching for reasons to put in effort. Even worse, they might find themselves searching for another job. In order to lift a team up, accomplishments must be recognized. Team members are acutely aware of each other's accomplishments, positive gestures, and support they have received. They are in a great position to recognize one another. This activity allows employees to demonstrate the appreciation they have for one another and recognize their peers for something specific. It also provides a space to discuss the importance of recognition in general.

Directions

1. Tell the group that one thing you'd like them to do today is find a fellow team member and thank them for a job well done.
2. Tell the participants to identify something specific to acknowledge—something they've noticed or heard.
3. Ask the participants for ways they can recognize their fellow team members.

Key Questions

- Why is it important to acknowledge and recognize each other?
- What are ways we can show recognition?
- What are some company programs that recognize great job performance?

Key Points

- Giving recognition helps us to feel valued and motivated to keep up the good work.
- By recognizing each other, it ultimately helps our customers.

Tips/Examples/Variations

Examples of specific recognition:

- "I admired how you remained cool under pressure with that unhappy customer."
- "You did a great job at meeting that deadline today. How did you do it?"
- "I like how you speak on the phone—your tone of voice is so upbeat and positive."

CATEGORY ► TEAM BUILDING

Purpose: To generate self-pride

Time Requirement: 10 minutes

Materials Needed: Paper and pens

While external recognition can be a powerful motivator, internally recognizing the worth of our work is just as important. It is easy to be hyper-critical of our own performance, especially if we deeply care about the work we are doing. On the surface, this "never good enough" attitude might seem like a motivating force. In the short term, it may be. In the long term, however, it is demoralizing. Self-deprecating lines of thought lead to fatigue and impact morale. The activity that follows expresses the value of self-recognition while allowing employees to practice the skill. Break the mindset of self-deprecation. Build a mindset of self-appreciation.

Directions

1. Say that it is motivating and helpful to receive recognition from each other but it is also important to give ourselves recognition for the work we do.
2. Tell the group to stand up.
3. Tell them to raise one hand.
4. Tell them to take that hand and put it on their back.
5. Tell them to pat their back a few times.
6. Say that they deserve to pat themselves on the back for the good work they do here!

Tips/Examples/Variations

Examples of other ways to give ourselves recognition:

- Take a break if we need one.
- Buy ourselves a nice lunch after a hard morning.
- Treat ourselves to a walk outside on a nice day.

CATEGORY ► TEAM BUILDING

Purpose: To identify ways to motivate each other

Time Requirement: 15 minutes

Materials Needed: Flipchart or whiteboard; markers

Your team is your support network. Strong support networks lift each other up when morale is low. It is important to recognize that behavior and outlook are infectious. One positive employee can change the entire culture of a team and subsequently the course of the project. In this way, supporting fellow team members is both selfless and self-serving. Great team members lift one another up! How can we actively practice encouragement in the workplace? The following activity opens that important discussion.

Directions

1. Tell the group that one way to show we believe in each other is to motivate each other when our motivation is low—like a personal cheerleader.
2. Ask for a volunteer. Tell the volunteer that they are going to role-play an employee who is having a bad day. The rest of the group will play themselves and offer ways to motivate, encourage, and support the employee. (This exercise should last five minutes.)
3. Have the volunteer leave the room and walk back in as the employee who is having a bad day.
4. Tell the group to try different ways to support and motivate the volunteer. Tell the volunteer to respond to the suggestions.
5. Debrief the discussion by using the **Key Questions** and **Key Points** that follow.

Key Questions

- Sometimes we feel low motivation because of something not tied to our job. How can this affect us when we are at work?
- Ask the volunteer: What made you feel better? What did the group do that truly motivated you? What did they do that was de-motivating?
- Ask the group: "What do you think worked well?"

Key Points

- We can motivate each other by offering supportive words, listening actively, offering to help, and brainstorming options to move forward.
- Be careful of saying "I understand" unless you've been in that situation before.
- Don't de-motivate the employee by talking about your problems instead of theirs.

Tips/Examples/Variations

Examples of how to motivate each other:

- Help out if a team member is overwhelmed.
- Recognize a team member for a job well done.
- Encourage a team member to continue his or her good work.

CATEGORY ► TEAM BUILDING

Purpose: To identify stress relievers to use on the job

Time Requirement: 10 minutes

Materials Needed: Index cards and markers

Deadlines, difficult customers, and other factors can raise anxiety in the workplace. Stress is just part of the job (any job, really). It cannot be avoided. That being said, our reaction to stress can make or break company success. Instead of allowing stress to mount up over time until we crack, it is productive to employ healthy coping mechanisms to mitigate the effects of workplace stress. Everyone has their own strategies to combat stress, and it can be helpful to share those strategies with coworkers. Certain tactics may have never occurred to members of the team, while others may learn about a tactic they like better. The following activity creates a conversation that helps team members identify more productive ways to address stress and find the relief they desire.

Directions

1. Introduce the exercise by saying that it is easy to get stressed when dealing with customers and our other job responsibilities.
2. Hand out an index card to each participant.
3. Ask them to write down one thing they do to overcome stress on the job. Examples could include: deep breathing, visualization, talking to a coworker, or taking a walk.
4. Collect the cards and discuss each stress-reducing idea with the group.
5. Ask each participant to try one of the ideas on the cards next time they feel stressed.

Key Questions

- What causes stress for you on the job?
- What are ways you deal with that stress productively?
- What stress busters might you find helpful?

Key Points

- It is normal to experience stress on the job, particularly with jobs dealing with customers.
- Customer service jobs require patience, and stress can try our patience.
- Many times, our customers come to us dealing with their own stress and will transfer it to a team member because that's how the customer is trying to deal with stress.
- There are many ways to deal with stress productively; try different ways until you find the ones that work for you.

Tips/Examples/Variations

Examples of ways to relieve stress:

- Take a walk.
- Take a coffee break.
- Go to a quiet place and breathe deeply.
- Call a friend for support.

CATEGORY ► TEAM BUILDING

Purpose: To help participants recognize and appreciate their strengths

Time Requirement: 10 minutes

Materials Needed: Flipchart or whiteboard; markers

Each member of a team possesses different strengths. Capitalizing on these strengths ensures that the team will thrive. It is important for individuals to recognize what they bring to the table. If they do, they can not only lean into these strengths, but use them to support other team members who might have complementary weaknesses. Cooperation and collaboration are keys to success, support, and growth of the team and its members. The activity below allows employees to visualize, identify, and subsequently articulate their strengths.

Directions

1. Ask participants to quickly brainstorm all the different items that people store in their kitchen drawers. Record them on the flipchart/whiteboard (i.e., knives, spatula, bottle opener, spaghetti spoon, whisk, vegetable brush, etc.).
2. Ask each participant to pick an item/utensil that best describes them—their strengths, styles, best characteristics.
3. Ask for volunteers to share their responses.
4. Use the **Key Questions** and **Key Points** that follow to debrief the activity.

Key Questions

- What did we learn about our teammates?
- How can we use our strengths to improve our team? Our work?
- How specifically can we use our strengths to help our customers?

Key Points

- Many of us focus on our weaknesses when, in fact, focusing on what we do well will help us perform better.
- Having diverse strengths on our team makes us stronger and more effective.
- Each of us brings important contributions to our team and our work; we would not be as successful if we all shared the same strengths and weaknesses.

Tips/Examples/Variations

Examples:

- Knife: Smart.
- Spaghetti spoon: Able to do a lot of things at once.
- Whisk: Able to work quickly and with energy.

CATEGORY ► **TEAM BUILDING**

Purpose: To help participants appreciate what they do well and to motivate them to continue these behaviors

Time Requirement: 10 minutes

Materials Needed: Flipchart or whiteboard; markers; paper and pens

I t is all about the little things. Small behaviors we have can greatly impact the experience of a customer. Whether it was being friendly or just ever so slightly going the extra mile, customers and coworkers notice. Oftentimes, though, customers do not provide feedback (positive or negative). Customers simply comment by continuing or ceasing their patronage. Coworkers express feedback through collaboration or the lack thereof. As such, it can be easy to overlook the little things we do well because they are not verbally recognized. The following exercise is designed to remind us about the importance of the little things. Our actions are seen and appreciated, even if not commented on. We always do better when we focus on our strengths.

Directions

1. Tell the participants that they will be writing a letter to another team member from a customer.
2. Each letter should highlight several things they do well and how their actions impressed the customer.
3. Give the participants a template of what the letter could look like (see next page) and record it on the flipchart or whiteboard.
4. Give them five minutes to write their letters.
5. Have volunteers share their letters.
6. Debrief using the **Key Questions** and **Key Points** that follow.

Key Questions

- How did your actions help and/or impress your customer?
- How did it make you feel to "get" this letter?
- What can you do to continue demonstrating these behaviors?
- Where do we find letters from our customers?

Key Points

- Remember—you do a lot of things well!
- These may seem like little acts to you but they leave the customer with strong, positive impressions.
- We have the opportunity to celebrate a team member's small act of kindness every day by reviewing the customer feedback.

Tips/Examples/Variations

- Here is an example of what a customer letter might look like:

Dear (team member name):

I wanted to write you to thank you for the service you provided recently at our company. You helped me _____.

Because of your help, you made me feel _____.

CATEGORY ▶ **TEAM BUILDING**

Purpose: To explore ways to address work challenges by taking small steps

Time Requirement: 15 minutes

Materials Needed: Flipchart or whiteboard; markers

Sooner or later, we all must face challenges in the workplace. Ideally, we rise to these challenges, overcome them, and are stronger for the experience. Oftentimes, however, these barriers seem too difficult or time consuming to address at any given moment. It can be tempting to put them off, especially when we have bigger fish to fry. If we do not address challenges, though, they tend to grow and overwhelm us later. When challenges arise, they must be addressed, no matter how daunting they appear. The key is to break these barriers down and tackle them little by little. Do you have a large stack of papers that need reading and sorting? Start with five, not the stack. Your odds of success increase exponentially. The following activity addresses this tactic and allows employees to explore it for themselves in order to improve productivity and reduce procrastination.

Directions

1. Introduce the topic by saying that we all face challenges in our jobs.
2. Ask the group to share honestly (with no repercussions) some of the barriers they are facing to doing their job well.
3. Say that we often don't address problems because they seem too big but if we break the solution into small steps, it is more achievable.
4. Ask the group to share small ways they could start to address your challenge.

Key Questions

- What gets in the way of us addressing work challenges?
- How can we use small steps to address challenges?
- What's one small step you'll take this week to address your challenge?

Key Points

- It's easier to address challenges if we break the solution into small steps.
- Often, once we start to take action, it becomes easier to solve the problem.

Tips/Examples/Variations

Examples of taking action:

- Break the problem into smaller tasks and do the hardest first.
- Break a problem into smaller steps and have each team member take a step.

CATEGORY ► **TEAM BUILDING**

Purpose: To discuss and appreciate the work of another group or department

Time Requirement: 10 minutes

Materials Needed: A tray with 15–20 random small items on it covered with cloth so that the team cannot see the items at first (examples: paper clip, mug, picture frame, keys, etc.); slips of paper; and pens

Companies are composed of many teams in many departments. We often think about our immediate team and forget about the role other teams in other departments play in the big picture. These departments work in tandem with one another to help the company function, and because of this each department is integral to the company's overall success. Having a greater understanding of each department fosters respect for their work, promoting a fuller company culture. It also promotes innovation, support, and cross-team collaboration.

Directions

1. Give the team 10 seconds to look at the tray uncovered.
2. Then give them 60 seconds to write down as many items as they remember seeing on the tray. The person who remembers the most items wins a prize!
3. Tie this in to the other department by making the point that the other department is responsible for many details and must remember so many things throughout each day.

Key Questions

Choose random team members to answer the following:

- What would you say are the top three most important aspects of your job?
- Describe an average workday for you.
- What do you find to be the most challenging aspect of your job?
- What things could other departments do to help you do your job more effectively?
- What are some important ways our team impacts our customers?

Key Points

- Every team is important to our customers. Certain teams represent the first as well as the last impression that our customers have of our company.
- We all must juggle many tasks while working under busy and stressful conditions.
- We have to be good at just about everything because at some point we will be called to do, or at least know the answer to, almost everything imaginable.

Tips/Examples/Variations

- Conduct today's team meeting near or in another department to gain their perspective.

CATEGORY ► TEAM BUILDING

Purpose: To recognize leadership in others

Time Requirement: 15 minutes

Materials Needed: Yarn (20+ ft.)

Contrary to popular belief, leadership is not a stagnant, set position. All employees find themselves in the leadership seat at some point or another. Maybe a coworker spearheaded a project. Maybe another took the lead on researching new tools for office management. While these examples do not come with an official leadership title, they are prime examples of it. Leadership and initiative should be encouraged and recognized but also shared. True leaders feel comfortable stepping out of the spotlight from time to time. The following activity helps your team see the leadership qualities in others, setting an example of recognition, collaboration, and leveraging everyone on the team.

Directions

1. Explain to the group that when ducks fly in a V formation, they share the leadership position at the tip of the V. Today we are going to recognize others for taking a leadership role.
2. Instruct the group to sit in a circle and to recognize a member of the team for a time when they exhibited leadership. When this happens, have the recognized team member hold a piece of yarn and pass the bundle to the next recognized team member.
3. Each team member will continue this process, choosing a team member who has not been recognized until everyone has been recognized and everyone in the group is connected.
4. Debrief using **Key Questions** and **Key Points** that follow.

Key Questions
- Why is it important for us to recognize the leadership qualities in others?
- How can we recognize leadership in others?
- What can we do to encourage others to be leaders?
- How can we learn how to be a better leader from others?

Key Points
- True leaders are comfortable both inside and outside of the spotlight. They can stand out or blend in depending on the situation.
- Proven leaders can help developing leaders identify opportunities to practice leadership.
- Part of being a leader is developing new leaders and passing our skills on to others.

Tips/Examples/Variations
- Challenge team members with more leadership experience to mentor developing leaders.

CATEGORY ► **TEAM BUILDING**

Purpose: To discuss how change affects our lives

Time Requirement: 10 minutes

Materials Needed: 3 pennies from different years (less than 20 years old)

The world is an ever-shifting landscape. Nothing stands still. Nothing is certain beyond the promise of change. Nobody is the same person now that they were yesterday, let alone a year ago. It is important to analyze how change has shaped us as individuals. What have we learned? Were we resilient? This reflection can only be done through taking a look back on our own lives, or else it becomes a theoretical conversation. The following activity helps employees take that tangible leap of reflection into their own past, hopefully providing insights about our future.

Directions

1.   Ask the group for three volunteers.
2.   Give a penny to each of the volunteers and instruct them to take note of the year.
3.   Ask each volunteer to share what they were doing during that point in their lives and describe how things have changed since then.
4.   Debrief using **Key Questions** and **Key Points** that follow.

Key Questions

•   What changes would you like to make in the year ahead?
•   Why are these changes important to you?
•   What can you start doing today to make those changes possible?

- What do you want to change that you've been putting off? Why?
- What obstacles are keeping you from making positive changes in your life?

Key Points

- Growth is the result of changes we make in our life.
- Change requires us to be flexible in order to adapt.
- Change keeps us from getting stuck in a rut.
- The best way to meet change is head-on.

Tips/Examples/Variations

- For a variation, have everyone in the group participate in the exercise.

Purpose: To examine our habits

Time Requirement: 10 minutes

Materials Needed: None

People are comprised of habits. Both positive and negative, they inform who we are and our behaviors. They dictate how we navigate the world around us. Since habits hold so much significance to our daily lives, self-improvement often involves the altering of our daily habits. How can we ax negative habits and replace them with positive ones? It all starts with identifying what our habits are to begin with, even the ones that are unintentional. Once we have done that, we can begin forming an action plan toward self-improvement.

Directions

1. Introduce today's topic by saying: You are your habits. Most of life is habitual. You do the same things you did yesterday, the day before, and every day for the last month. Habits, good or bad, make you who you are.
2. Ask the group to think about a bad habit they have had in the past.
3. Ask for three volunteers to share a bad habit that they overcame, how they overcame it, and how changing that habit affected their lives.
4. Debrief using **Key Questions** and **Key Points** that follow.

Key Questions

- What are some good habits that can impact how productive and effective we are at our jobs?
- Why is it so important for us to be aware of and work on our bad habits?
- What's the best way to eliminate bad habits?

Key Points

- Building good habits such as eating a healthy breakfast, getting enough sleep, being on time, and being well organized will help us be more productive and effective in our work.
- Bad habits can be contagious and infect the entire team. When we develop bad habits at work, everyone suffers, including our customers.
- The only way to eliminate bad habits is to replace them with good ones. It takes 21 days to create a new habit.

Tips/Examples/Variations

Here are some tips when you are trying to establish a new habit:

- Commit to at least 30 days, every day.
- Start simple—do something that you can stick to easily without a lot of thought.
- Write it down—having your new habit goals written on paper is important; share with others.
- Remove temptation—make sure that you are set up to win!
- Remind yourself—put notes everywhere. Tell others so they can help.

CATEGORY ► **TEAM BUILDING**

Purpose: To share and take pride in our accomplishments

Time Requirement: 10 minutes

Materials Needed: None

What does it mean to take pride in your accomplishments? On the surface, it may seem as though taking pride in our accomplishments is like recognizing ourselves. It may even feel egotistical. That is far from the truth. The fact is, taking pride in our work is so much more than a self-provided pat on the back. Taking pride in our accomplishments helps us see our value, as well as the value of our work. This, in turn, boosts motivation and moves us toward success. Pride is different from arrogance. One is earned, the other is a cover to hide weaknesses. The following activity opens up a discussion about pride and how we can cultivate it in our work.

Directions
1. Ask team members to share their personal definition of pride.
2. Ask each person on the leadership team to talk about the specific accomplishments of the team this year—the things the team should be proud of.
3. Applaud the team after each one.
4. Spend time as a leader telling the team how proud you are of their specific accomplishments, both collectively and as individuals.

Key Questions
- How does pride affect our attitude toward our work?
- Why is it important for us to take pride in our work?

- Do you take pride in what you do for your customers every day?
- Do you take pride in your team's accomplishments?

Key Points

- Having a sense of pride about who you are and what you do is essential to success. This doesn't mean arrogance or denying your weaknesses. A healthy sense of pride is a good thing.
- Taking pride in our work helps us to be more engaged and creates a home atmosphere for our customers.
- It is important that you recognize your progress, take pride in your accomplishments, and share your achievements with others. Brag a little and feel good about what you have done so that you can go on to do even more!

Tips/Examples/Variations

- *Pride:* A sense of one's own proper dignity or value; self-respect.

CATEGORY ► TEAM BUILDING

Purpose: To discuss how we want to be perceived and recognized by others

Time Requirement: 10 minutes

Materials Needed: None

People always have a perception. It is impossible for a customer to look at a company and not form an opinion. Executives are sizing up who is ready to move up in the organization, leaders are looking to see who can take on more responsibility, and so on. These opinions and judgments are based on several factors. How was their experience? What do they think about the ethics of the company? Were they satisfied with the product? However, these opinions and judgments can be altered if we focus on how customers perceive our company. To do this, we have to establish what experience we want customers to have and then move toward that goal. It all starts with identification. What do we want to be known for? What improvements can we make? The following activity opens up the discussion in order to establish a plan of attack.

Directions

1. Conduct today's exercise: "Let's Give Them Something to Talk About."
2. Say: "Today we are talking about how we can help identify the things that we want others to say about us and our culture. Imagine that two years from now a major magazine decides to do a feature story on our company. They are interested in writing about our culture and the major improvements we've made over the past two years."

3. Present the discussion: "Our story should be titled _____
    because we _____."

Key Questions

- What do we want to be known for?
- How can we influence what others say about us?
- What are some things that we need to work on that would wow others?
- What major improvements could we make within two years?
- What are some small things we can do today and every day thereafter that would add up to huge results two years from now?

Key Points

- People are going to talk about us regardless of what we do, but what they say is up to us.
- Major improvements take time and require consistent effort.

Tips/Examples/Variations

- Ask the group to give some examples of things they would not want others to be saying about us.

CATEGORY ► **TEAM BUILDING**

Purpose: The importance of preparation

Time Requirement: 10 minutes

Materials Needed: None

Stay on your toes! It can be easy to fall into complacency when we find ourselves in a comfortable routine, especially when times are good. However, we must remain alert, constantly searching for avenues to improve the experience for our customer. Becoming complacent only leads to one place: mediocrity. Growing too comfortable leaves room for drops in quality and motivation. Taking time to prepare helps us perform better and make fewer mistakes. Work life has become so fast paced that we can find ourselves running from one task or project to another without proper preparation.

Directions

1. Have everyone stand in a circle with a leader in the middle.
2. Begin by teaching the group the various poses of the game. There should be at least five. (See the examples on the next page to get you started or have team members demonstrate their favorites.)
3. When a leader points to a person in the circle and calls out a pose, they must strike that pose quickly and correctly. If someone messes up, makes the wrong pose, or moves when they were not supposed to, then they are out. You be the judge.
4. Tie it in by saying that being prepared helps us to be sharp mentally, ready to take on any challenge.
5. Debrief and discuss **Key Questions** and **Key Points** that follow.

Key Questions

- What are some things you need to do in your position to prepare to take great care of our customers every day?
- What kinds of things can get in the way to keep us from being prepared?

Key Points

- The more prepared you are, the better your chance for success.
- Laziness, apathy, being late, and distractions from home are just a few of the things that keep us from being prepared.
- There is preparation that needs to be done in every area that touches our customers.

Tips/Examples/Variations

Examples of poses (you can make up your own):

- The ape: Have them pound on their chest and make ape noises and then unpeel a banana.
- The bunny rabbit: Have them put their paws up, make their teeth look like buck teeth, and hop once.
- The tiger: Have them crouch down, roar, and claw the air.
- The Abe Lincoln: Have them pound a pretend podium and say "four score and seven years ago."

Purpose: To define what "We Deliver Small Acts to Make a Big Difference" means

Time Requirement: 10 minutes

Materials Needed: Flipchart or whiteboard; markers

We hear a lot of talk about the "big picture" these days. These are the large, foundational cornerstones of a company—the product and the vision. While the big picture is integral to the function of a company, it isn't the entire picture. Success lies in the small acts. Small moments of going above and beyond make all the difference to customers and coworkers, setting you and the company apart from competitors. While it has become somewhat clichéd, "service with a smile" is well known for a reason. For a restaurant, the big picture may be the food. However, the smile sets that particular establishment apart. What small acts can we incorporate into the workplace?

Directions

1. Ask the group what they think is meant by "We Deliver Small Acts to Make a Big Difference."
2. Ask for ideas as to what small acts we could do to make a difference in our workplace.
3. Facilitate and debrief using the **Key Questions** and **Key Points** that follow.

Key Questions

- What small acts have you received as a customer?
- How did it make a difference in your experience?
- What are some small acts we can do here to make a difference?

Key Points

- It's often the small acts that we remember as customers.
- Small acts make us stand out from our competitors and could be the key reason customers are loyal to our company.
- Small acts add up over time.

Tips/Examples/Variations

Examples of small acts:

- Holding the door open.
- Offering to carry a bag.

CHAPTER 6

UNCOVERING SOLUTIONS

CATEGORY ► **PROBLEM SOLVING**

Purpose: To define what "Involve Your Team in Making Improvements" means

Time Requirement: 10 minutes

Materials Needed: Flipchart or whiteboard; markers

What does it mean to make improvements to a company? How do we tackle such a vague goal? Who is involved in this process? In order to improve a company, we have to identify the benefits of any proposed improvement. Nobody knows the operations of a company better than the employees. It would seem crazy to make major decisions without their input, wouldn't it? Unfortunately, this practice happens often. Employees feel valued when their feedback is taken into account. They become part of the solution. Moreover, they likely hold insights to the problems facing the company that can only be seen from their perspective. The following activity is designed to open that important conversation.

Directions

1. Ask the group what they think "Involve Your Team in Making Improvements" means. Record their answers on the flipchart/whiteboard.

2. Ask them how we benefit when the entire team is involved in making improvements.
3. Ask them how it makes them feel when they are involved in a decision and are part of the solution.
4. Say that the goal of this exercise is for us to come up with ideas, find solutions, and work toward common goals as a team.
5. Say that it is important for each of us to stay open-minded about suggestions and to be creative and think outside the box.
6. Summarize the discussion by using the **Key Questions** and **Key Points** that follow.

Key Questions

- What does "Involve Your Team in Making Improvements" mean?
- Why is it beneficial to involve everyone?
- How do we feel when we are included in decision making and problem solving?

Key Points

- "Involve Your Team in Making Improvements" means that managers don't just tell team members what to do but find ways for team members to be involved.
- It is beneficial to get everyone involved because it allows for a variety of ideas and opinions and creates accountability for problems, decisions, and solutions.
- We feel valued and important when we are asked for our opinion and are included in problem solving.

Tips/Examples/Variations

Examples of how we benefit when the entire team is involved in making improvements:

- We share the responsibility for making changes so one person doesn't carry the burden.
- We feel a sense of ownership and pride when we all work together to make improvements.
- When the entire team is involved, we have access to a lot of different ideas and opinions, which may help us make the improvement more easily.

CATEGORY ► PROBLEM SOLVING

Purpose: To practice keeping an open mind to the opinions of others

Time Requirement: 15 minutes

Materials Needed: None

People view the world with different eyes. As such, opinions are bound to clash at some point. Opinions are often tied to a person's identity and ego, making discussions difficult. When disagreements occur in the workplace, we can view it in one of two ways: as a problem or an opportunity to grow. We'd like to choose the latter. To do this, though, empathy must be employed. People have a tendency to grow defensive on topics they care about; they dig into their opinions. Instead, we need to try to approach diversity of thought with an open mind. The following activity is a great exercise in openness and understanding. It isn't about sacrificing your own vision, but about genuinely hearing other visions out.

Directions

1. Start the activity by posing a provocative question to the group. Pick a topic that elicits a variety of opinions, but nothing too controversial. (You can use the sample questions on the next page.)
2. Ask for a volunteer to share their views on the question/topic.
3. Ask for a show of hands as to who agrees/disagrees with the volunteer.
4. Pick one person who has disagreed with the volunteer and ask them to state their views. Then ask them to find one thing the volunteer said that they agree with.
5. Pick another person in opposition to the volunteer's opinion and ask them to pick one thing they agree with.

6. Continue the activity until various views are stated. Encourage the group to see the positive in every opinion.

7. Summarize the activity by using the **Key Questions** and **Key Points** that follow.

Key Questions

- Why is it important to be open about others' opinions?
- How can we keep an open mind?
- How does keeping an open mind benefit the team and our work?

Key Points

- Everybody has opinions, and every opinion holds some truth and has value.
- It's important to find the truth in every opinion and to try to understand why others have the opinions they do.
- Teams are strengthened by a variety of ideas. Keep an open mind and it will help you be more understanding, flexible, and creative.

Tips/Examples/Variations

Sample questions:

- Should all restaurants be completely nonsmoking?
- Should speed limits be raised across the country?
- Should schools be open (with students in attendance) year-round?
- Should checkout be 10 a.m.?

CATEGORY ▶ PROBLEM SOLVING

Purpose: To empower the team to help you make a decision

Time Requirement: 10 minutes

Materials Needed: Flipchart or whiteboard; markers

Together, a team is stronger. When we face challenges at work, it can be easy to try and tackle our problems alone. Maybe we don't want to appear incapable. Maybe we don't want to burden other members of the team. Either way, by acting alone, we negate a major resource we have—the people we work with. Getting together and brainstorming solutions to problems often presents options we never knew were available to us. We also generate buy-in, develop our people, and create a culture of problem solving along the way. This cooperation is the lifeblood of a company.

Directions

1. Prior to this activity, think of a challenge you are facing in your job. Choose one that you can share with your team and one that has a variety of possible solutions.
2. Introduce the topic by telling the group that you have a real-life work challenge or decision that you are facing and you'd like their input.
3. Share the challenge/decision with them. Write it on the flipchart.
4. Ask the group to brainstorm ways to deal with this challenge or ideas on what decision to make. Tell the group that there is not a "wrong" answer so they can feel free to respond.
5. Ask the group to help you narrow down some choices.
6. Debrief the exercise by using the **Key Questions** and **Key Points** that follow.

Key Questions
- How did brainstorming help us in this situation?
- How might brainstorming help us on the job?
- Why might we want to get team input on decisions or challenges we are facing?
- What might be some disadvantages to getting everyone's opinion?

Key Points
- Brainstorming solutions and ideas helps us think creatively about how to address a situation and capitalize on the knowledge and experience of the team.
- Others might have had this same experience before and can share what they did and how it worked.
- Involving the team helps us feel supported when we are facing challenges and decisions.
- We may not want to use brainstorming for every decision we make; it could overwhelm us with too much information in the case of a simple decision.

Tips/Examples/Variations
- A variation is to have a participant pose a challenge they are facing and have the rest of the team members come up with ideas. Examples of decisions you could share with the group include a procedural change or a new customer policy.

Purpose: To discuss how to get our customers involved in making improvements

Time Requirement: 10 minutes

Materials Needed: Flipchart or whiteboard; markers

When improving the company, the customer should be kept in mind. Their input is paramount when deciding new directions, especially since the customer is an essential party to the company's success. How can we effectively implement customer input? Customers often have the best feedback, as they live the customer experience. They see a perception of the company that is unique to them, uninfluenced by inside knowledge and experience. The following exercise allows an opportunity to brainstorm on this very topic. If you do not work directly with customers, this activity can be adjusted to focus on internal customers.

Directions

1. Introduce the topic by saying that it can be helpful to involve our customers in making improvements.
2. Ask the group to brainstorm ways to involve our customers in making improvements. Record the ideas on the flipchart or whiteboard. Don't censure any ideas at this point.
3. Ask the group to narrow down the list to the one idea that they'd like to start working on now.
4. Write the words *What, How, Where, When,* and *Who* vertically on the flipchart to establish an action plan to implement the idea.
5. Fill out each component for the idea. Summarize by saying we'll see how we're doing with the plan at a future meeting. Set the meeting date.

Key Questions

- Why do we want to involve our customers in making improvements?
- What resources do we have to tell us how our customers feel about us?
- How can we involve our customers in making improvements?
- Why is it important to get their input?
- How will asking customers for suggestions increase morale, customer feedback, and profits?

Key Points

- Customers often have great ideas for how things could be improved because they live the customer experience.
- We may not see things as subjectively as customers do so it's helpful to get their perspective.
- We can involve our customers by asking for their opinions, having them try out a new procedure, or running a new idea by them.
- Customers feel special and cared for when we involve them.

Tips/Examples/Variations

Examples for how to involve customers:

- Ask for their opinions and feedback on a new process or procedure.
- Have a contest for the customers to give suggestions for improvements.

CATEGORY ▶ PROBLEM SOLVING

Purpose: To empower the team to identify and make improvements

Time Requirement: 10 minutes

Materials Needed: Index cards (either 3" x 5" or 4" x 6"); pens

Organizations are structured by nature. Most utilize hierarchies and matrices to manage people, processes, and goals. Sometimes team members lose sight of the idea that they can make decisions, find solutions, and more. This activity reminds employees that they have the power to improve the team, company, and the way we deliver our goods and services. Determining what we have control over helps each of us to deliver every day. While this activity focuses on customers, it can be adapted to use for internal issues and internal customers.

Directions

1. Ask the group to imagine that they make the rules for how we treat customers.
2. Break the group into smaller groups of two or three people.
3. Give each group three index cards.
4. Tell them to create one rule (for each card) that they might establish for how to serve our customers better.
5. Encourage them to be as specific as possible; for example, answer the phone within three rings, and so on.
6. Give the group five minutes to come up with the three rules.
7. Reconvene the group and ask them to share their rules. Record them on the flipchart/whiteboard.
8. Debrief by asking the **Key Questions** and **Key Points** that follow.

Key Questions

- What are ideas that can be implemented right away?
- What ideas need approval from others?
- What ideas do we want to start with?

Key Points

- We have the power as a team to make some of these changes.
- Management appreciates and needs our input because we deal with the customers every day.

Tips/Examples/Variations

- A simple variation is to have them brainstorm three ideas without index cards and then share them with the larger group.

CATEGORY ▶ **PROBLEM SOLVING**

Purpose: To practice thinking outside the box

Time Requirement: 10 minutes

Materials Needed: None

I n order to improve, we have to try what has not been tried. This involves generating ideas that are outside of our comfort zone. This is the epitome of thinking outside the box. We can never move forward if we are unwilling to think creatively. Sometimes, we avoid new ideas or creative solutions because we have become too comfortable or are afraid of the unknown. The hard truth is, the devil you know is NOT better than the devil you don't. While exploring the unexplored carries risk, it also harbors the opportunity for advancement—something that staying still does not. The following activity is designed to promote creative thinking in a workplace context.

Directions

1. Ask the group what "thinking outside the box" means.
2. Ask how thinking outside the box can help us make improvements.
3. Facilitate the discussion by using the **Key Questions** and **Key Points** that follow.
4. Tell the group that you'd like them to think outside the box for one problem they face today.
5. Ask them to share their results with another team member.

Key Questions

- What does "thinking outside the box" mean?
- How can thinking outside the box benefit our team and our organization?
- Why don't people think outside the box?

Key Points

- "Thinking outside the box" means looking for new ways to address a problem or handle a situation rather than relying on tried and true methods.
- Thinking outside the box can help our team work more creatively and may help us better address problems we face.
- Sometimes people don't think outside the box because they are afraid or are too comfortable with "business as usual."

Tips/Examples/Variations

Examples of thinking outside the box:

- Revisiting a previous idea that was not given a lot of consideration.
- Asking for feedback from team members who normally are shy or hesitant to offer ideas.
- Looking at a problem from another point of view (a customer, a staff person not associated with the problem, etc.).

CATEGORY ▶ **PROBLEM SOLVING**

Purpose: To practice handling the suggestions of others

Time Requirement: 15 minutes

Materials Needed: Flipchart or whiteboard; markers

In order to make improvements, we must be open to suggestions. Sometimes, it can be easy to assume that we have all of the answers. However, better options for advancement and growth are often found through collaboration. Two heads are better than one, after all. The following exercise explores openness to suggestion. Additionally, it provides a framework for accepting good ideas and respectfully declining ideas that need to be reworked. The last thing we want to do is shut somebody down. Our ability to work with and from others' ideas can be a real difference maker.

Directions

1. Say that in order to make improvements, we have to be open to the suggestions of others.
2. Ask why we may be "closed" at times to suggestions.
3. Say there is a four-step process that will help us stay open to suggestions (write these steps on the flipchart/whiteboard):
   a. Thank the team member for thinking of new ideas.
   b. Consider the idea before making comments.
   c. If the idea will work: involve the team member.
   d. If the idea does not work: encourage the team member to continue sharing ideas.

Key Questions

- How does it help our team and our work to be open to the suggestions of others?
- Why may we be "closed" to suggestions at times?

Key Points

- Being open to the suggestions of others may help generate new ideas and ways to make improvements.
- Sometimes we are "closed" to suggestions because we think we know best or don't want to take the time to hear others out.
- Using the four-step process—especially "considering the idea before making comments"—may open the door to new ways of thinking and problem solving.

Tips/Examples/Variations

- This can be a more in-depth exercise by having team members practice the four steps. Break them into pairs. One person will share a problem, the other will offer suggestions. Instruct the person with the problem to practice using the four steps to help them stay open to suggestions.

CATEGORY ▶ **PROBLEM SOLVING**

Purpose: To develop a vision for improvements to work situations

Time Requirement: 15 minutes

Materials Needed: Flipchart or whiteboard; markers

Every advancement starts with a vision. If we want to build a better company culture, the ideal must first be seen. Without this crucial step, any advancements will not be cohesive. They'll lack direction. In order to work toward something, you must know what that something is. The direction of a company isn't necessarily one person's vision. We must all connect to the broader vision provided by leadership. This is why the following activity asks the entire team to visualize their ideal work situation and then brainstorm the steps they need to follow in order to usher those concepts into reality.

Directions

1. Ask the group to visualize what their ideal work situation would look like in one year (at their current job).
2. Ask for volunteers to share their ideal.
3. Ask the group for ideas on how they could achieve some components of the ideal.
4. Ask: "How can we continue to do the things that are working well?"
5. Ask: "How can we work toward the ideal?"
6. Record their responses.

Key Questions

- What things would we keep the same?
- What things would we change?
- How can we maintain the things that are going well?

Key Points

- It is important to recognize and appreciate that many things are working well.
- We can change the things that are not working—the first step is identifying what they are.

Tips/Examples/Variations

- A variation is to go around the room and ask each team member for one thing they'd do to improve the workplace. Discuss.

CATEGORY ▶ PROBLEM SOLVING

Purpose: To identify time wasters

Time Requirement: 10 minutes

Materials Needed: Flipchart or whiteboard; markers

Time wasters are ineffective practices we use to put off work. This can come in the form of distractions or inefficient work habits. Time wasters are, generally speaking, an avoidance tactic. We might not always be aware of when we use them, either. In order to eliminate them, we must first recognize when we are employing them. The following activity allows employees the opportunity to learn about time wasters as well as identify them in their own lives in order to find more productive approaches.

Directions

1. Introduce the topic by asking: "How can eliminating time wasters be an act that makes a big difference?" Discuss.
2. Break the group into small teams. Give them each a piece of flipchart paper.
3. Give them five minutes to come up with a list of time wasters they see or experience on the job.
4. Reconvene and have each team review their responses.
5. Debrief by using the **Key Questions** and **Key Points** that follow.

Key Questions

- What are time wasters?
- Why do we want to eliminate them?
- How can we eliminate them?

Key Points

- Time wasters are inefficient ways we do our work or avoid doing our work.
- Time wasters take our focus away from our work and take up our energy.
- We can eliminate them by becoming aware of when we waste time and substituting a different way to do our work.

Tips/Examples/Variations

Examples of time wasters:

- Talking on the phone with friends.
- Surfing the internet.
- Not doing tasks right the first time.

CATEGORY ▶ PROBLEM SOLVING

Purpose: To define ways to demonstrate a can-do attitude

Time Requirement: 10 minutes

Materials Needed: Flipchart or whiteboard; markers

Great team players exhibit a can-do attitude. When challenges arise and stress begins to mount, keeping a positive and solution-oriented outlook can be the difference between success and failure. This attitude radiates throughout a company, elevating the culture to new heights. In turn, this radiates outward to customers, who take notice. To be can-do oriented is to be solution oriented, positive, and proactive. This mindset can be applied to any situation at work, which is why the following activity centers on can-do application. What does *can-do* mean to us? How can we apply it daily? What effects will it have on our work?

Directions

1. Ask the participants what they think a can-do attitude means in terms of our jobs.
2. Record their responses on the flipchart/whiteboard.
3. Ask the group to think of ways they could show a can-do attitude on the job.
4. Record responses on the flipchart.
5. Facilitate the discussion by using the **Key Questions** and **Key Points** that follow.

Key Questions

- What does demonstrating a can-do attitude mean?
- What are ways we can show we have a can-do attitude?
- What gets in the way of us having a can-do attitude?

Key Points

- Having a positive attitude is an important component of excellent customer service.
- Often, things like stress and other tasks get in the way of demonstrating a can-do attitude.
- Having a can-do attitude makes you a good team player and makes our jobs more enjoyable.
- Customers can recognize a can-do attitude and appreciate all you do even when it's not perfect.

Tips/Examples/Variations

- Examples: *Can-do* can mean being proactive, taking initiative, doing something with a smile, and offering to help without being asked.

CATEGORY ► **PROBLEM SOLVING**

Purpose: To examine different ways to solve problems

Time Requirement: 15 minutes

Materials Needed: Different hats—enough for everyone in the room

Keeping an open mind allows us to approach problems more effectively. When we keep an open mind, two things happen: we are able to collaborate and we are able to consider options we previously would not have. Just because we find one solution to a problem does not mean that it is the best solution. Working as a team allows us to generate more ideas. With more options, we can weigh the best way to proceed. Not all solutions are made equally and we vastly expand our arsenal of fixes when we keep an open mind. Exploring multiple approaches drives a richer understanding and possibly new ideas through co-creation and co-discovery.

Directions

1. Introduce the topic by saying that there is often more than one solution to a problem.
2. Ask for a volunteer to share any work-related challenges he or she is facing or a problem that needs to be solved.
3. Hand out the hats so that each participant is wearing one of them.
4. Go around the room and ask each participant for one idea on how to address this problem.
5. Now tell them to switch hats so they are wearing a new one.
6. Say that now that they are wearing a new hat, they need to consider another way to solve this problem.

7. Go around the room again with each participant sharing one idea.

8. Debrief the exercise by using the **Key Questions** and **Key Points** that follow.

Key Questions

- What happened when you switched your hat?
- Why is it helpful to get input from everyone on the team?
- Why is it helpful to keep an open mind when solving a problem?

Key Points

- Keeping an open mind may help us approach problems more effectively.
- Getting various opinions may help us when we're stuck.
- Use all your human resources when problem solving; be creative.
- Measure your success via customer feedback.

Tips/Examples/Variations

- If you cannot get enough hats, you can have the participants pretend they are switching hats.

Purpose: To examine our problem-solving styles and how they contribute to the team in order to improve customer feedback

Time Requirement: 15 minutes

Materials Needed: Flipchart or whiteboard; markers

Everyone has different values that inform the choices they make and how they choose to address problems. Sometimes, values between people complement each other. Other times, it can be a source of disagreement. How can we use these different perspectives to our advantage? Instead of being a source of conflict, differing values can be an asset to a team. The following exercise allows employees to explore their differing viewpoints through a lighthearted question. Afterward, they have the opportunity to justify their choices and discuss how their varying viewpoints can work to the benefit of the team. Sometimes the "why" people choose is more important and insightful than the choice itself.

Directions
1. Tell the participants to imagine that they are marooned on an island.
2. Ask them to identify three items they would bring if they knew they were going to be stranded.
3. Say that they can only pick three items total for the group.
4. Tell the group they have five minutes to identify the items.
5. Once they are finished, ask them to defend their choices.
6. Facilitate a discussion by using the **Key Questions** and **Key Points** that follow.

Key Questions

- Why did you pick that item?
- Was there agreement on this item? Why or why not?
- How did you come to agreement if there were differences of opinion?
- How can you use that same problem-solving strategy on the job?

Key Points

- We all have different values; they are neither good nor bad, just different.
- Can you see how what we do needs to be what the customer wants?
- Different values add to the power and effectiveness of the team.
- We may have differences of opinion, but we can work through them via communication and discussion.
- Leverage these differences to get another perspective.

Tips/Examples/Variations

- An option is to have them select fewer items (one or two) if you want to encourage more debate and teamwork skills.

CATEGORY ► PROBLEM SOLVING

Purpose: To examine ways to fix things we'd like to change

Time Requirement: 15 minutes

Materials Needed: Flipchart or whiteboard; markers; something that could serve as a "magic wand" (i.e., a ruler, a stick, a pen, etc.)

Sometimes, when things aren't working, it can be easy to just accept them as a necessary evil of the job. This isn't always true. Most everything is subject to some degree of change, and challenges we face can be altered in order to be more efficient or enjoyable. Since we have a tendency to ignore and accept our current reality, we can sometimes choose frustration in our job when it is unnecessary. This activity allows employees to think about areas of their job that they would like to improve and then helps set up a framework toward positive change.

Directions

1. Begin the exercise by saying that you've found a magic wand. Say that the magic wand will allow you to change one work activity.
2. Pass the wand around and have each participant share the one thing they'd like to change. Write their answers on the chart.
3. Facilitate a discussion by using the **Key Questions** and **Key Points** that follow.

Key Questions

- Why did you choose this one thing you'd like to change?
- Imagine the magic wand has lost its power. What can you do to implement the change? Can you keep doing it consistently?
- Is it a change within your control or someone else's control? What can you do about that?

Key Points

- Many times, we have the power to change things we are not happy with.
- Making improvements starts with taking action, whether it be communicating the problem or participating in solving the problem.
- If we all took some ownership of the problems we face, we would have fewer challenges to face.
- It's easier to focus on the problem than the solution. Be a part of the solution instead.
- Own the problem and don't give it back the way you got it.
- Check for satisfaction with your customers when you solve a problem; check with teammates when you change a process.

Tips/Examples/Variations

- An option is to have them pick the work activity they'd like to change, and before they discuss it have the wand lose its power. This would encourage them to "focus on solutions" and take responsibility for change.

CHAPTER 7

PRIORITIZING SAFETY

CATEGORY ► SAFETY FIRST

Purpose: Accident prevention

Time Requirement: 10 minutes

Materials Needed: None

Accident prevention is essential to a healthy office culture. Guidelines and procedures are put in place to ensure safety; however, they have a tendency to be dry. Sometimes they can even seem arbitrary. When these rules seem arbitrary, people relax on their adherence to them. An unsafe office ceases to be a productive or healthy office. How can we drive home the importance of safety guidelines? The following activity is designed to bring accident prevention to a real place, reminding employees what is at stake and why accident prevention is such a necessity.

Directions

1. Gather your team in a half-moon (semicircle) format.
2. Ask: "Who did you say goodbye to when you left home this morning?"
3. Listen to several responses and then use them in your next statement.

4. Say: "I want you to think about how _____ would feel if I had to call them and tell them you were in an accident."
5. Debrief and discuss the **Key Questions** and **Key Points** that follow.

Key Questions

- Ask: "How can you make accident prevention a part of your daily routine?"
- What kinds of things can get in the way of us being prepared?
- Do you point out unsafe areas of the operation if you notice them?
- Tie back to above by asking, "How would you feel if you ignored something and someone later got hurt as a result of this?"

(Use as many suggestions provided by your team as possible from the above questions.)

Key Points

- The more prepared you are, the better your chance of avoiding an accident.
- Ensure your tools are in good condition.
- Stick to guidelines and procedures.
- Never cut corners.
- Report unsafe conditions to your supervisor if it is something you can't safely handle.

Tips/Examples/Variations

Examples

- You can also have each team member write down suggestions for you to pull randomly from a hat and read if you have team members that don't speak up in a group.

CATEGORY ▶ SAFETY FIRST

Purpose: To practice putting out potential fires

Time Requirement: 10 minutes

Materials Needed: Two buckets with confetti inside—this activity will need to be done in a meeting room or outside where there is plenty of room to move and the space can be easily cleaned up

A traditional part of accident prevention involves theory and protocol. Reviewing safety procedures in concept does not always resonate with employees, nor does it accurately predict what an individual will do if placed in a genuine emergency. When the heat is on, people tend to forget the safety packet that was handed out at the beginning of the year. Instead, it can be more engaging to review safety procedures tangibly. The following activity allows employees to get on their feet while reviewing safety procedures. Crafting an engaging experience is far more likely to promote procedure retention.

Directions

1. Break the group into two teams.
2. Create a "fire" a few feet ahead of each team's starting position.
3. Have each person on the team run to the "fire" and put it out using a little bit of confetti, making sure to leave some for the rest of the team, then run back and tag the next person.
4. Award a prize to the team that puts out the "fire" first.
5. Review the following safety procedures with the team:
   a. Location of the emergency shutoff valve.
   b. Fire alarm evacuation.
   c. Fire extinguisher procedures.

Key Questions

- How well do you feel prepared to handle a potential fire?
- How prepared are we as a team to deal with emergencies such as fire?
- How do you think you would respond if there was a fire today? Would you react calmly and with clear direction, or panic?

Key Points

- Dealing with an emergency can be extremely stressful and even confusing. Being effective requires a firm knowledge of what to do.
- Luck runs out, but safety is good for life.

Tips/Examples/Variations

None.

CATEGORY ► **SAFETY FIRST**

Purpose: Staying hydrated

Time Requirement: 10 minutes

Materials Needed: None

Drink up! It seems simple, but staying hydrated can prevent a majority of heat-related illnesses, especially if the work involves physical labor or is in a location without fantastic ventilation. This activity is a review on the importance of hydration. It delves not only into hydration, but why hydration is important. The conversation extends beyond hydration as well. This is a matter of self-maintenance. Taking care of ourselves impacts our work, our alertness, and our health. How can we remember to take care of ourselves consistently?

Directions

1. Gather your team in a half-moon (semicircle) format.
2. Ask: "How many of you have ever suffered from a heat-related illness?"
3. When someone raises their hand or responds, ask, "How did it make you feel?"
4. Say: "Summer is approaching fast and we need to be prepared so we can avoid these types of illnesses."
5. Debrief and discuss **Key Questions** and **Key Points** that follow.

Key Questions

- Ask: "What causes dehydration?"
- Ask: "When is it important to drink water to prevent this from occurring?"
  - Most people don't realize it is the amount of water you drink several hours prior to work that prevents dehydration.

- Ask: "How do you know the proper amount of water to intake daily?"
  - A simple formula is to divide your body weight in half and that is the number of ounces you should drink daily. Example: If you weigh 200 lbs., you should drink 100 ounces of water a day. That is 8½ glasses of water!

Key Points

- Drink even when you are not thirsty.
- Have a routine when it comes to hydrating.
- Have a tall glass of water first thing every morning.

Tips/Examples/Variations

Examples

- You can also have each team member write down suggestions for you to pull randomly from a hat and read if you have team members that don't speak up in a group.

Purpose: To discuss accident prevention and incident reporting

Time Requirement: 10 minutes

Materials Needed: Flipchart or whiteboard; markers

Cause and effect. The process in which our actions in the present influence the future is not always clear to us. Only in hindsight can we clearly see how 1 + 2 made 3. This is the core of accident prevention. Prevention is the act of taking precautions, even when it might seem excessive. It helps us account for unknown future variables. That chair left in the hallway caused someone to trip and fall. More likely than not, nobody had predicted that chair would result in an accident. This is why preparation and prevention is important. Because of the "what-ifs." The following activity allows employees to brainstorm possible accidents and how to prevent them.

Directions

1. Break the team into three small groups.
2. Assign each group an area of the company.
Example areas:
   - Housekeeping area
   - Common area
   - Kitchen/Breakroom
   - Parking lot
   - Storage rooms
3. Direct each group to brainstorm potential dangers and accidents in their area.

4. Instruct each group to determine what the team can do to prevent these potential hazards.
5. Review the following company safety procedures with the team:
    a. Incident Reporting Procedures—both associate and customer incidents
    b. Slip and Fall Prevention

Key Questions

- How many on-the-job accidents have we had this year at the company?
- When was the last time we had an accident? What happened? Could it have been prevented?
- What precautions do you take to ensure your safety at work?

Key Points

- Most accidents are preventable.
- A moment of carelessness can lead to an accident, but prevention is a full-time job.
- Prevention can be as simple as being mindful while we work and knowing the proper procedures.
- Danger never takes a vacation.

Tips/Examples/Variations

- Have each department compete to be accident-free for the year and offer a prize to each department that keeps the pledge.

CATEGORY ► SAFETY FIRST

Purpose: Discuss emergency procedures with the team

Time Requirement: 10 minutes

Materials Needed: A small bowl filled with long-grain rice, blindfolds, and a few packages of very small (the baby-size) safety pins

Safety doesn't happen by accident. A safe environment is a proactive one. Concentration is required to uphold safety in the workplace. Too often, people assume that safety involves avoiding unsafe choices. In truth, office safety revolves around making active, safe choices, such as keeping the office clean, reviewing safety procedures, and so on. This is an active mindset that requires mindfulness. The following exercise promotes and explores how concentration and safety are inseparably linked.

Directions

1. Instruct the group to sit in a circle.
2. Have each person use a blindfold (or watch them to make sure they don't look down into their bowl).
3. Ask participants to take turns trying to pick out as many baby safety pins as they can in 30 seconds.
4. The person who picks out the most wins. It's difficult to do—the baby pins feel exactly like the rice.
5. Explain to the group that on-the-job safety involves focus and concentration on each task, just like the exercise above.
6. Review the following company safety procedures with the team:
    a. Emergency contact list and call protocol.
    b. Power outage and storm procedures.
7. Debrief using **Key Questions** and **Key Points** that follow.

Key Questions

- What are some ways that we could get injured on the job?
- What can we do to contribute to a safer work environment?
- How can we provide a safe environment for our customers?

Key Points

- Safety doesn't happen by accident; it involves conscious, consistent effort.
- Knowing safety procedures is the best way to ensure a positive outcome during emergencies.
- Having a clear understanding and knowledge of what to do during an emergency will help us avoid panic and allow us to perform under pressure.

Tips/Examples/Variations

- Variation: Quiz team members on various safety procedures to see what they know and to identify areas that need work.

CHAPTER 8

SERVING YOUR CUSTOMER

CATEGORY ► CUSTOMER SERVICE

Purpose: To come up with ideas for small acts participants can do to please the customer

Time Requirement: 10 minutes

Materials Needed: A Koosh ball, potato, or regular ball (or a crumpled piece of paper)

How can we improve the experience for our customers? It is easy to get caught in the rut of usual ideas. But what if we want to go above and beyond? In order to think outside the box, we have to silence the voice in our head that might immediately shoot down new ideas. The following activity doesn't give us time to self-censor. Instead, it promotes spontaneous idea generation. There isn't enough time to say *this won't work* or *what a bad idea*. Not all ideas will be winners, but the few that are gold can push the customer's experience from good to great. This activity can be adapted for internal customers as well.

Directions

1. Introduce the topic by saying that we're going to come up with as many small ways to please the customer as possible—by playing "hot potato."
2. Say that we're going to pass around the "potato" and have only a second or two to come up with one small act.
3. Start the exercise. Encourage the participants to come up with ideas quickly—no right or wrong answers!
4. End the exercise once enough ideas are generated—a few go-arounds.
5. Instruct the group to pick one of the ideas and try it with a customer today.

Key Questions

• What are small ways we can please the customer?
• Are our ideas realistic and easy to do?

Key Points

• There are many small and quick ways to please the customer.
• It doesn't require a lot of energy to have great results with the customer.

Tips/Examples/Variations

Examples of small ways to please the customer:

• Say a friendly "welcome."
• Say a genuine "thank you."
• Acknowledge something they said about their day.

CATEGORY ▶ CUSTOMER SERVICE

Purpose: To identify good telephone etiquette

Time Requirement: 10 minutes

Materials Needed: Two toy telephones or cutouts of telephones

Whether we answer the phone when an external customer calls, an internal customer calls, or we are talking with a partner, vendor, or supplier, we make an impression. Our ability to handle phone calls professionally impacts our relationships inside and outside the company. This activity is a good reminder that our attitude and manners are reflected in our phone conversations. Without a physical presence and facial expressions, our tone of voice, enunciation, and other verbal cues play a larger role. Developing stronger phone habits and etiquette is more important than we typically acknowledge.

Directions
1. Have two people act out a possible phone conversation.
2. Debrief the call and identify the call positives as well as the challenges.
3. Ask the group how stellar telephone manners can help make a big difference in the service we offer to our customers.
4. Be sure to review and discuss "Tips for good phone manners" listed on the next page.

Key Questions
- Why do we want to practice excellent phone manners?
- How does poor phone etiquette reflect on our business?

Key Points

- Much of our business is conducted over the phone. It's as important as our face-to-face interactions.
- Poor phone manners reflect badly on our company and can be frustrating for customers.
- When we pick up the phone, it may be the customer's first experience with us and therefore his or her first impression of us.

Tips/Examples/Variations

Tips for good phone manners:

- Say your name when you answer the phone.
- Use the customer's name in the conversation.
- Avoid putting callers on hold for too long.
- Ask callers if they mind being put on hold.
- When transferring calls, let the caller and the receiver know that you are transferring a call.
- Speak clearly, loudly, and slowly.

CATEGORY ► CUSTOMER SERVICE

Purpose: To help participants appreciate how specific small acts can impact customer experience / business goals

Time Requirement: 10 minutes

Materials Needed: Flipchart or whiteboard; markers

Making a difference for internal or external customers doesn't require an exorbitant amount of resources. It can feel like elevating a customer's experience requires lots of time, money, and ingenuity. However, the little things can radically impact a customer's visit just as much as major gestures. A pleasant attitude, attentiveness, and care cost nothing but surely resonate with customers. Little things, like keeping customer spaces clean or inquiring as to whether customers need help prior to their asking, can change their experience entirely. The following exercise focuses on the little things. How can we elevate the client experience on a daily basis, in small ways?

Directions

1. Instruct the participants that they will have "homework" between now and the next meeting.
2. Their homework is to identify three small acts in their day-to-day life as a customer that made their lives easier or more pleasant.
3. Tell them they can look for these small acts when they go to the grocery store, dry cleaner, restaurant, or wherever else.
4. At the next meeting, ask the participants to share their three acts.

Key Questions

- What was one small act that you experienced?
- How did that make your life easier or more pleasant?
- Is that particular act something we could do here?

Key Points

- It doesn't take a lot of energy, or cost money, to have great impact.
- There are many small acts one can do—be creative!
- Remember how it feels to be a customer and what a difference small acts can make.

Tips/Examples/Variations

- Have the team members look for things such as how they were greeted, how they were appreciated for their business, whether their business was taken care of easily and quickly, and so on.

CATEGORY ► CUSTOMER SERVICE

Purpose: To examine our biases and first impressions based on appearances

Time Requirement: 15 minutes

Materials Needed: Five pictures of people from magazines— pick pictures that show a diverse population, types of dress, and so on; do not use pictures of famous people

People form snap judgments. It is human nature to do so. Snap judgments limit our ability to openly engage coworkers and customers. In order to mitigate the effects of our biases, we must first be aware of them. The following exercise allows employees to think about their own biases and preconceived notions. Bias is a balancing act, as we can control our own preconceived notions, but we cannot do the same for our customers. How can we influence our customers' perceptions of us? These are all important questions to ask when engaging with customers internally or externally.

Directions

1. Introduce the topic by saying that we often form first impressions of people based on appearances. These first impressions can be inaccurate or unfair.
2. Show one of the five magazine pictures. Pass it around if necessary.
3. Ask the group what their impression is of this person and why they have this impression (there are no right or wrong answers).
4. Discuss how first impressions can impede our interactions with our customers and that we have to watch how we treat others based on appearances.

5. Say that we also have to consider what impressions WE send by the way we dress (for example, wearing our uniform correctly).

6. Debrief the activity by using the **Key Questions** and **Key Points** that follow.

Key Questions

*   How can our first impressions affect our interactions with our customers?
*   What can we do to make sure we don't let our first impressions impact our customer relationships?
*   How can WE create a better first impression for our customers?

Key Points

*   First impressions are powerful.
*   Be careful what judgments you make about our customers based on appearances.
*   Examine what first impression we are sending with the way we look and dress.
*   Remember, "you can't judge a book by its cover."

Tips/Examples/Variations

*   Example: A customer comes in with wrinkled and dirty clothes and his shirt untucked. We could make a first impression that this customer is disorganized or may not be able to pay. We may learn that, in fact, this customer may have just left work at a construction job.

CATEGORY ▶ CUSTOMER SERVICE

Purpose: To examine solutions to customer complaints

Time Requirement: 10 minutes

Materials Needed: Flipchart or whiteboard; markers; paper and pens

We need to track trends in order to get an accurate picture of our company from the outside. What are our customers saying? Do they have any complaints? If so, we should identify what the most common complaints are in order to address them as soon as possible. Discussing complaints and their subsequent solutions is a group effort, as everyone has likely encountered their own experiences with unsatisfied customers. By sharing these experiences with one another, the group can see the larger trends at play. The following activity provides a space for these topics to be discussed. This activity can be adjusted to internal customer situations as well.

Directions

1. Introduce the topic by asking the participants to think about the top complaints they hear from customers.
2. Hand out an index card to each of the participants and ask them to record two complaints they hear.
3. Ask for volunteers to share their responses and record them on the flipchart or whiteboard. Identify the top three complaints.
4. Identify the top complaint.
5. Focusing on one complaint at a time, ask the group for ideas on how we could use this complaint as an opportunity.
6. Use the **Key Questions** and **Key Points** that follow for discussion and debrief.

Key Questions

- What are the most common complaints we hear?
- How can we use these complaints to improve?
- What opportunities do you see in these complaints?
- How can we turn these complaints around to please our customers?

Key Points

- Good customer service involves effectively addressing customer complaints.
- In each customer complaint, there's an opportunity for us to improve or change the way we do things.
- We can measure our problem resolution by looking at the customer feedback.

Tips/Examples/Variations

- Customer feedback measures problem resolution—do we meet customer needs or exceed them?

CATEGORY ► CUSTOMER SERVICE

Purpose: To help participants build rapport with customers

Time Requirement: 10 minutes

Materials Needed: Flipchart or whiteboard; markers

Relationships take customer service to the next level. As a customer, feeling like you know the company you're working with heightens the experience. When the relationship between customer and company becomes more personal, trust is formed and customers feel important. This is why we build rapport with customers, to help establish these relationships. In order to build rapport, we have to put effort into our body language, our tone, manners, and small talk. These small actions change the tone of a business transaction entirely. It's more than just business. It's about relationships. These skills matter internally in an organization as well. The following exercise allows employees to discuss the importance of rapport, as well as how to build it.

Directions

1. Introduce the topic by asking the participants, "What does building rapport mean?"
2. Ask them why building rapport is important to do with our customers.
3. Have the group brainstorm ways to build rapport with the customer and record their answers on the flipchart/whiteboard. Answers could include:
   a. Saying "please" and "thank you."
   b. Demonstrating positive body language to show you are listening, such as nodding, smiling, and so on.
   c. Using the customer's name.

    d. Being empathic to a customer's situation.

    e. Acknowledging their feelings.

    f. Engaging in small talk about the weather, sports teams, travel, and so on.

Key Questions

- How does building rapport make a customer interaction more memorable?
- In which customer interactions could we use rapport-building techniques?

Key Points

- Building rapport makes interactions with customers more memorable and pleasant.
- There are many simple ways to build rapport.
- We measure our effectiveness via our relationships with our customers.

Tips/Examples/Variations

- A variation is to have two participants role-play an interaction with a customer based on a scenario you give them. Note the positive things the team member did to build rapport. Note the words they used as well as their body language.

CATEGORY ► CUSTOMER SERVICE

Purpose: To define ways to "go the extra mile"

Time Requirement: 15 minutes

Materials Needed: Flipchart or whiteboard; markers

Why is it important to "go the extra mile"? It can be easy to think that the bare minimum gets the job done. Why not do the job the simplest way possible with minimal effort? It might seem like, as long as the job gets done, the amount of effort involved is not all that important. This is a dangerous line of thinking that leads to sloppy work, poor morale, and a lack of pride in work. If we neglect to go the extra mile, the job may still get done, but the customer won't be swept off their feet. In fact, they might not return. This is because "the extra mile" is what sets your company apart from competitors. It shows care. The following exercise opens a space to discuss going the extra mile in the context of your specific workplace. Remember that we should make a difference in every interaction we can.

Directions
1. Introduce the topic by asking the participants what "go the extra mile" means in terms of customer service.
2. Break the group into two groups and tell them to come up with a list of two to four ways that explain how they could go the extra mile with our customers.
3. Reconvene the group and ask for volunteers to share their ideas.
4. Record their responses.

5. Facilitate and debrief the discussion using the **Key Questions** and **Key Points** that follow.
6. Instruct the participants to pick one of the examples shared and use it sometime this week.

Key Questions

- What does "go the extra mile" mean?
- How can we go the extra mile with our customers?
- How does going the extra mile spotlight our customers?

Key Points

- "Go the extra mile" means taking more steps to try to please the customer and going out of our way to make them happy.
- There are many ways to go beyond typical service and leave the customer with a memorable experience.

Tips/Examples/Variations

Examples of going the extra mile:

- Phone a customer to make sure everything is satisfactory.
- Write a customer a handwritten thank-you note for their business.
- Gift customers a gift card as a sign of appreciation.
- Be a sounding board for a client, even when there is no business in it for you.

CATEGORY ▶ CUSTOMER SERVICE

Purpose: To identify a variety of ways to spotlight the internal or external customer

Time Requirement: 15 minutes

Materials Needed: Flipchart or whiteboard; markers; paper and pens

Customers are individuals, and individuals deserve special attention. When building a productive company culture, we have to find ways to put the spotlight on the customers. Generally, everyone knows that the customer is important on a theoretical level, but what does it look like to live out that principle? Do we know the names of our clients? What does our rapport look like? Do we go the extra mile? Do we recognize what our better relationships look like and how they were developed? The following activity creates a space for the team to identify ways that they put the spotlight on the customer.

Directions

1. Introduce the topic by saying that there are many ways we can spotlight our customers and show we care.
2. Say that we're going to do an activity that will encourage us to be creative about how to spotlight the customer.
3. Give each participant a piece of paper.
4. Tell them to write their name vertically (up and down) on their paper.
5. Say that you want them to think of one way to spotlight our customers using at least three letters of their name (you can share the example on the next page).
6. Give them five to ten minutes to complete the exercise.

7. Reconvene and have each participant share what they came up with.
8. Tell the group that you will collect their papers, summarize all the ideas, and send them the summary.
9. Debrief by using the **Key Questions** and **Key Points** that follow.

Key Questions

- What does "spotlight the customer" mean?
- Why is that important to our business?
- How can we spotlight our customers?

Key Points

- "Spotlight the customer" means you pay close attention to individual customer needs, you help customers see how valued they are (recognize), you develop a connection with customers (using their name, anticipating what they need), and you ensure customer satisfaction and positive customer feedback.
- There are many ways to spotlight our customers. Try new ways to make connections and let them know how valued they are.

Tips/Examples/Variations

- **S**—Show kindness.
- **T**—Tell them about a new service or feature.
- **E**—Explain directions clearly.
- **P**—Pick a return customer and give them special attention.
- **H**—Help customers that are struggling with their luggage.

CATEGORY ▶ **CUSTOMER SERVICE**

Purpose: To identify who our customers are

Time Requirement: 15 minutes

Materials Needed: Flipchart or whiteboard; markers

What is a customer? Well, you could say a customer is a person who purchases goods and services from another. However, in a broader sense, a customer is someone who relies on us for a service. In this sense, there are two types of customers: internal and external. External customers are outside of our organization, likely the people who come to mind when the question was initially asked. Internal customers are people who rely on us from within our organization. These are coworkers, team members, different departments, and so on. These internal customers must be given the same care and attention as our external customers. If members of an organization don't treat one another well, the external customer will suffer. The following activity introduces this concept and opens a discussion about its importance.

Directions

1. Introduce the topic by saying that we have many different customers we deal with daily.
2. Ask the group: "What is a customer?"
3. Say that the official definition of *customer* is "a person who purchases goods or services from another," but we'll use the word *customer* to describe people who rely on us for a service.
4. Break the group into two teams. Tell them that they will be given five minutes to come up with a list of who their customers are.
5. Reconvene the group. Ask them to share their answers.
6. Say that some customers are "external customers," and some are "internal customers." External customers are people outside the

organization who rely on us, and internal customers are people within the organization who rely on us.

7. Say that our customers would fall in the category of external customers.

8. Ask the group what would happen if we didn't treat our internal customers as well as our external customers.

9. Say that it is critical that we treat each other well because if we don't, the customers will suffer.

Key Questions

- What is a customer?
- What is the difference between an external customer and an internal customer?
- Why should we treat our internal customers as well as our external customers?

Key Points

- A customer is defined as someone who relies on us for goods or services.
- An external customer is one outside the organization—such as our customers.
- An internal customer is one inside our organization—such as coworkers.
- We should treat our internal customers as well as our external customers.
- If we don't treat each other well, our internal system falls apart, making it difficult to offer great service to our customers.

Tips/Examples/Variations

- Example: An internal customer in housekeeping needs to know when customers need assistance. She waits for that information from another internal customer. That information is not shared promptly. Frustration and anger result, and the needs are not met. The external customer suffers when their needs are not met. The internal customers suffer because their working relationship is hampered.

CATEGORY ► CUSTOMER SERVICE

Purpose: To discuss the differences between us and our competition

Time Requirement: 10 minutes

Materials Needed: Flipchart; markers

To get ahead of the competition, we need to offer an experience and a service that is unique from our competitors and needed by our customers. In order to continue improving our services, we have to keep a finger on the pulse of our industry. What are our competitors doing to better compete with us? What are similar departments or functions in other companies that we respect doing? What makes us unique? How can we lean into that? When it comes down to it, the dedication of employees is what ultimately sets companies apart. It is the work done by individuals at the company that pushes the customer to return instead of leaving for a competitor. It is important to discuss this concept with the team, which is exactly what this activity aims to accomplish. Benchmarking, even on an informal level, is a helpful activity.

Directions

1. Explain to participants that as a company we offer a unique service and experience for our customers. Since we opened our doors, others have tried to adopt our model.
2. Ask the group to identify some of our competitors. Record on the flipchart.
3. Ask the group how to discuss in what way these companies are competing with us and why we are a better choice for customers.
4. Debrief using the **Key Questions** and **Key Points** that follow.

Key Questions

- Who are our competitors?
- What sets us apart from the competition?
- How can we out-serve our competition?
- Do we take our competitors seriously?
- How is this particular company unique?

Key Points

- While our brand and amenities can help to set us apart, it is people like you who make the real difference.
- Better customer service is how we as a staff create value and loyalty for our customers.
- As a company, we offer a different service and a different experience than our competition.
- Every time a customer needs company service, they have a choice to make and it's our job every day to give our customers more reasons to continue choosing us.

Tips/Examples/Variations

- Variation: Ask participants to explain why they would tell their family members to choose our company.

CATEGORY ► CUSTOMER SERVICE

Purpose: To review and celebrate leads and revenue; to reinforce the sales and service connection with all team members

Time Requirement: 10 minutes

Materials Needed: None

How can we provide value for our customers? The dedication of individuals greatly improves the customer's experience. Sometimes, it can be beneficial to recognize that impact directly. The following exercise is an opportunity not only to recognize employees who have been impactful, but to explain how their work has directly moved the company toward its goals. This brings the theoretical into a tangible space. If this activity proves difficult, work hard to find the connections that do exist.

Directions

1. Give a business update.
2. Share goals as a business.
3. Celebrate and recognize team members who have positively impacted those goals.
4. Use awards for special milestones.
5. Conduct the following exercise:
    a. Say: "Today we are talking about providing value to our customer. We're all going to help think of ways to increase value for our customers."
    b. Present the discussion: "I can increase our value for customers by _____."

Key Questions

- How does personalized customer service in this area help "sell" our business?
- What are different ways team members' personal experiences could help increase our value for the customer?
- How does personalized customer service in this area promote customer loyalty?

Key Points

- Every team member can use personalized customer service as a way to build customer loyalty and encourage word-of-mouth referrals from customers.
- Remember, every decision we make needs to keep our customers in mind.
- Each action we take should strengthen our customer relationships.

Tips/Examples/Variations

- Example: "I can increase value by providing helpful information to our customers."

Customer service comes in many forms. As such, it is productive to constantly brainstorm new ways to improve the customer experience. The following activity allows employees to reflect on that important issue through a tangible experience. This aids in unconventional idea generation. No idea is inherently off limits. Even the simple, small gestures can make a customer's day, so don't write off proposals on the basis of their simplicity. After a period of idea generation, open a discussion on how some of the ideas can be implemented. This is a team process. Remember, customer service can be focused internally or externally.

Directions

1. Tell the participants that they will select an item out of the bag and relate that object to a service or team improvement that could be made.
2. Show them an example. Take a paper clip and say: "This paper clip makes me think about being organized. Maybe we could be more organized about how we check in with our customers."
3. Start the activity. Have each participant select one object and relate it to a customer service improvement, as above.
4. Debrief by using the **Key Questions** and **Key Points** that follow.

Key Questions

- How did this exercise help us generate ideas?
- How can we implement the ideas?
- What other ideas do you have regarding a service or team improvement?

Key Points

- Brainstorming solutions and ideas to common work issues helps us think outside the box and draws on the creativity and knowledge of the group.
- Even small changes can make a huge difference in a customer's experience.
- Remind the group of the tools they have.

Tips/Examples/Variations

- A variation is to use one object, such as a paper clip, and have each participant come up with something different related to a customer service improvement.

CATEGORY ▶ CUSTOMER SERVICE

Purpose: To recognize our customers' contribution to our success

Time Requirement: 10 minutes

Materials Needed: Flipchart or whiteboard; markers

Customers are an integral piece of a company's ecosystem. Without them, the entire model would fall apart. In a way, they are part of the team. Just as we recognize members of our teams, build them up, and reward them, we should do the same for customers. How can we work to make the customer feel special and essential? This activity provides a space to discuss customer recognition. How can we take the customer experience to the next level? Think about internal customers as well.

Directions

1. Ask why it is important not only to recognize each other but to recognize how our customers contribute to our success.
2. Ask the group to brainstorm how we can recognize and reward our customers.
3. Debrief by using the **Key Questions** and **Key Points** that follow.

Key Questions

- How can we recognize our customers?
- Why do we want to recognize our customers?
- What service delivery tools do we have that help us recognize customers?

Key Points

- Recognizing customers helps them feel special and will encourage them to return.
- It's especially important to acknowledge our return customers; they are the meat and potatoes of our business.

Tips/Examples/Variations

Examples of how we can recognize our customers:

- Remember their preferences.
- Ask about their day.
- Thank them for choosing us.

Purpose: To make and keep promises

Time Requirement: 10 minutes

Materials Needed: None

A promise is a pledge, specifically a pledge to deliver on something. Companies, departments, and individuals make promises all the time. However, certain groups and individuals outline their promises more clearly and live up to those promises more consistently than others.

Directions
1. Ask the group why it is important to live up to your promises.
2. Ask for thoughts on the promises this company makes to its customers.
3. Discuss how the organization can better keep those promises.
4. Explore how each person on the team impacts customer experience.
5. Debrief the activity by using the **Key Questions** and **Key Points** that follow.

Key Questions
- How do we or can we measure our ability to keep our customer promise?
- How consequential is our promise and the experience our customers have?
- How much effort do our customers have to expend to do business with us? How much do we make our customers work?
- How does our customer experience compare with that of our competitors?

Key Points

- We need to differentiate ourselves through the customer experience.
- Each of us has an impact directly or indirectly on our customers' experience.

Tips/Examples/Variations

- Focus on internal customers and how it is to work with your department.
- Approach the activity by thinking about the experience of working with you as an individual. Do you create a great experience for your customers, internal customers, or coworkers?

► CONCLUSION

Good leaders translate culture and promote organizational values. The way they engage their team matters. Great leaders know this intuitively. Most meetings can be cancelled or skipped. They are a waste of time. Updates can be provided in so many other ways. Ad hoc meetings can be utilized for special circumstances with the appropriate people in them. Regular meetings should be short, reflect key activities, tie people to the business, connect one another, build comradery, engage your people, and sustain your desired culture. To do this effectively, it takes more than just standing up and delivering the same "one-way communication" message each day, week, or month. If you want your team to show up engaged and ready to perform at their best level, you as the leader must first show up and pull them in.

Every meeting should follow an agenda similar to the one we have provided. Let's quickly review the components.

Introduction: Provide purpose to the meeting and make sure your people are okay. How is the team functioning? How are people feeling? Are we at risk of losing anyone? This is your chance to show that people are your first focus. We say people are important, but do we demonstrate that by talking about it?

Past performance: Every employee should know where the business stands based on key performance indicators (KPIs). If the KPIs are on target, it is a quick review and an acknowledgment of what is working. If KPIs are off, the team may have ideas on how to address the gap. Regardless . . . share the numbers!

What is happening: All too often, team members are surprised by events, visitors, changes, and so on. This is the time to make sure people know what is coming up. This should be very short and to the point. Sometimes there may be little, or even nothing, to mention.

Culture building: This is probably the most important aspect of a meeting and the main purpose for the contents in this book. We should regularly build and sustain our culture using activities and discussions like the ones in this book. Make sure there is a bottom line or call to action to this section of the meeting.

Recognition: Find people doing good things. Celebrate them for the small and large victories. It is that simple. However, if you have developed a great culture, you will find that your employees will start to use this time to recognize one another. Now that is engagement!

Close: Make sure the end of the meeting is clear. Don't let it fizzle out. Remind people of the call to action and to be there for each other.

Once you have a cadence to holding these meetings, try letting team members run them. You can even create a rotation. They will make it fun and take on more ownership.

Think back in your career about the leaders you have followed. If you identify the traits of your great bosses and compare them to your not-so-great bosses, how did their communication styles differ? How did you feel when they delivered a message? What made the good leaders worth following? Which leader are you more like today? Which leader would you like to be in the future?

Being a leader in today's ever-changing work environment is not an easy task; however, the more engaged your team becomes, the easier your job as their leader will become. By using this book as a guide, you can become more effective with your messaging and, more importantly, your ability to engage your team and build the productive culture you desire. By doing so, you will notice an increase in the level of discretionary effort put forth by your team members. You will also notice that your team will feel more open to discussing problem areas within your organization as well as offering solutions for these problems.

Remember, if your people are important to you and your business success, then the people issues must be acknowledged, addressed, and discussed on a consistent basis. What you discuss is symbolic of what matters. If all you talk about is problems, then only problems seem to matter. What if you talked about trust, success, teamwork, leadership, and your customers on a regular basis? What if your team was a part of that discussion? Can you imagine what might be possible? Time to find out!

Have you been looking for a way to use current technology as a vehicle to cultivate your culture and drive engagement? How would you like to have a mobile companion that could provide you with additional impactful activities like those provided in this book, customized to your culture and values? Contact us today for more information on how to gain access to exclusive content through a convenient mobile application!

HUDDLE AGENDA

Introduction

Past Performance: *Share the numbers!*

	Previous Day	Month to Date	Goals

Note: *Remember to share what the numbers mean. What are the implications?*

What is happening? *Today's story:*

- ✓ Staffing
- ✓ Scheduling
- ✓ Sales
- ✓ Opportunities and Challenges

- ✓ Other
- ✓ _____
- ✓ _____
- ✓ _____

Culture Building:

Theme:

Activity/Discussion:

Call to Action *(Key lesson from Activity put to use with our customers)*

Recognition *(Who on the staff should be recognized and for what achievement?)*

Close

► ACKNOWLEDGMENTS

Throughout the years, certain people stand out because of the role they play in your life. I have been lucky enough to have three mentors in my life. Without their support and wisdom, I would not be where I am today. Thank you to Mike Michaelson, Dru Bagwell, and Neal Nadler. Know that in some not-so-small way you helped bring my career to this point and gave me the insights and support to create and finish an endeavor such as this.

To my team at PerformancePoint: I could not ask for a better team. I get to work with the best people. I look forward to continuing our efforts to "inspire others to discover and live their possible."

A special thank-you to my colleague Brian Poindexter, whose help on this book was invaluable.

► ABOUT THE AUTHOR

Every day, people wake up and trudge to work, resentfully working at a company that falls short of its promises and values. This is a problem that Brad Federman has dedicated his career to resolving. He is committed to helping organizations engage employees and customers and build resilient relationships, as well as creating collaborative and agile cultures.

As he puts it, his job is to "help organizations discover and live their possible."

This mission has followed Brad throughout his career as an international author, speaker, coach, and consultant with more than twenty-five years of corporate experience.

As the founder of PerformancePoint, Brad works with organizations and leadership in various industries, including household names such as Nordstrom, FedEx, Embassy Hilton, Mayo Clinic, Deloitte & Touche LLP, and Polo Ralph Lauren Corporation.

Prior to PerformancePoint, Brad was the EVP of Novations Group and has held leadership positions with Accenture and Humana Inc. He is a frequently requested featured speaker at conferences and business meetings worldwide. Some of his other works include *Employee Engagement: A Roadmap for Creating Profits, Optimizing Performance, and Increasing Loyalty*; *Jump Start: 50 Ways to Engage Your Team*; and, as a contributing author, *101 Ways to Enhance Your Career*. Additionally, Brad has been interviewed by Fox Business News's *Stossel* show and for articles in numerous publications such as *American Banker*, *Fortune Small Business*, the *Los Angeles Times*, and *HR Magazine*.

Brad earned his BA degree in communications from the University of Maryland and a MEd degree in human resource development from Vanderbilt University. He is also a member of the Forbes Coaches Council and serves on several boards.